M000311515

MESSING ABOUT IN BOATS

MICHAEL HOFMANN

MESSING ABOUT IN BOATS

OXFORD
UNIVERSITY PRESS

OXFORD

UNIVERSITY PRESS

Great Clarendon Street, Oxford, OX2 6DP,
United Kingdom

Oxford University Press is a department of the University of Oxford.
It furthers the University's objective of excellence in research, scholarship,
and education by publishing worldwide. Oxford is a registered trade mark of
Oxford University Press in the UK and in certain other countries

© Michael Hofmann 2021

The moral rights of the author have been asserted

First Edition published in 2021

Impression: 1

Published in the United States of America by Oxford University Press
198 Madison Avenue, New York, NY 10016, United States of America

British Library Cataloguing in Publication Data
Data available

Library of Congress Control Number: 2020952994

ISBN 978–0–19–884804–2

DOI: 10.1093/oso/9780198848042.001.0001

Printed and bound by
CPI Group (UK) Ltd, Croydon, CR0 4YY

To Mitzi Angel and Frederick Seidel

auf die Schiffe, ihr Philosophen!

—Friedrich Nietzsche

CONTENTS

INTRODUCTION

Ship of fools. Death ship, ark, ghost ship, slave ship, clipper, warship. Factory ship, trawler, galley, hulk. Lighter and collier and tug, aircraft carrier and tanker, container ship and banana boat. Dhow, pinnace, trireme, felucca, knar. Galleon, dugout, tramp steamer, raft. *Argo, Dawn Treader, Flying Dutchman, Pequod, Kon-Tiki. Nina, Pinto, Santa Maria. Mayflower.* Bogart and Hepburn's *African Queen*, Darwin's *Beagle*, St. Brendan's stone coracle with which he sailed to the Isle of the Blessed. The *Missouri*, the *Bismarck*, the *Ark Royal*, the *Mont Blanc*, the munitions ship that, with its unstable cargo of picric acid, TNT, and fuel oil, in 1917 blew up half of Halifax, Nova Scotia. The *Mary Rose*, the *Golden Hind*, the *Victory*, Géricault's *Medusa*, J.M.W. Turner's *Fighting Téméraire*. The *Titanic*, the *Windrush*, the *Herald of Free Enterprise*, the royal yacht *Britannia*. Classes of ship, actual ships, fictional ships, legendary ships. Their names, like the names of literary works, in italics. The *Bellerophon*, the *Erebus*, the *Endeavour*. Aircraft carriers and airports, in a recent development much to be deprecated, named for presidents and politicians. The Gerald S. Ford, as it might be, the Spiro T. Agnew. Masefield's 'Cargoes', Muldoon's 'Away and read Masefield's "Cargoes"'.[1] Ezra Pound's epic of the twentieth century, *The Cantos*, a poem containing history, beginning 'then went down to the sea in ships', Conrad's *Victory*, Katherine Anne Porter's novel *Ship of Fools*, with its passengers bound for Fascist or Fascescent Europe from Mexico, set in 1931, finally published in 1962. The Homeric prescription for Osip Mandelstam's insomnia, 'I have read halfway through the list of ships'. The unnamed ships of Baudelaire in 'The Albatross', of Coleridge in 'The Ancient Mariner'. The raggle-taggle improvised, co-opted navies evacuating at Dunkirk, mission-supporting in the Falklands, the *ex machina* ships that take away the trapped, unemployed, starving heroes of Hamsun's *Hunger* and Wolfgang Koeppen's *Youth*. 'What pretty names your ships have Lily Attentive Bulldog Trimmer Mastiff', the naïve breathless Sally writes from London to her Latin lover and revolutionary *in spe* General Francisco Miranda (more pretty names there, especially General) in V.S. Naipaul's *A Way in the World*; I am not sure if there are three or five of them, or two or four. Malcolm Lowry's *S.S. Plantagenet* in *Lunar Caustic*, 'that had suffered more accidents than any ship afloat', Gabriel Garcia Marquez's lovers' ship that hoists the yellow cholera flag to remain undisturbed, Alexander Trocchi's garbage scow in the waters of New York Harbor in *Cain's Book*, Kapuscinski's armada waiting, helpfully, fearfully, vulturishly, off the coast of Luanda—Luanda *delenda*, Angola—ready to take the white colonists and their crated chattels off to Rio or Lisbon and safety.

Ships have an amplitude and a containment and a definition that makes them naturally symbolic or expressive, at least as much as a town or house or horse or pet. Ships, not to be confused with, as Wikipedia says, boats. As much personality as a cat, as a Joseph Roth character remarks, of his horse. Cat-boats. Ship as individual. Ship as envelope with sender and addressee, ship as collective, as mission, as microcosm. Ship as vector and vessel.

A ship, as named and enclosed and burdened as a poem, as efficient and evocative as a postage stamp. Go, little book. Stay, moment, thou art fair. One of John Berryman's *Sonnets* (Sonnet 15), 'after Petrarch & Wyatt', sees the poet/lover as an allegorical ship:

> What was Ashore, then? … Cargoed with Forget,
> My ship runs down a midnight winter storm
> Between whirlpool and rock, and my white love's form
> Gleams at the wheel, her hair streams. When we met
> Seaward, Thought frank & guilty to each oar set
> Hands careless of poet as of the waters' harm.
> Endless a wet wind wears my sail, dark's swarm
> Endless of sighs and veering hopes, love's fret.
>
> Rain of tears, real, mist of imagined scorn,
> No rest accords the fraying shrouds, all thwart
> Already with mistakes, foresight so short.
> Muffled in capes of waves my clear sighs, torn,
> Hitherto most clear,—Loyalty and Art.
> And I begin now to despair of port.

When he brought out the second collection of Dream Songs, *His Toy His Dream His Rest*, Berryman chose an epigraph from the solo round-the-world yachtsman Sir Francis Chichester.[2] Habent sua fata naves—quite as much as the libelli do.

Casting about for a subject, among translating and writing and speech tones and prose and verse and various unmanageable categories and contentions for a long time, and arguments I could see myself advancing for maybe a sentence and a half, before petering out, looking up at you, with a shrug and 'Well?', I abruptly jibbed and thought: wrong. I want something contained. I don't want to nibble at an elephant, so let me strain at a gnat. Let me write what feels like a lot about a little. A single poem as subject, ergo four talks about four poems. I happened to half-remember Rilke's

'Auswanderer-Schiff', 'Emigrant-Ship', sub-headed Neapel, Naples, the way a ship bears the name also of its home-port: Freetown, or Dieppe or Veracruz. That gave me my theme and my start. A second would be probably the most famous one of these, though I hadn't read it for years: Rimbaud's 'Bateau Ivre', the 'Drunken Ship' (or 'Drunken Boat' according to Beckett). No getting around that one, if I could decide on which one. A third, 'sing softer', Montale's dreamy 'Barche sulla Marna', 'Boats on the Marne'. And a fourth, inscribing its thick, luxurious wake into the now, Karen Solie's 'The World'. Four talks on four poems in four languages. I could produce my German, resurrect my French, play make-believe with my Italian, and so give you my cut-rate impression of Stanley Burnshaw.[3] Four ships, four talks, four adventures.

RAINER MARIA RILKE

'Auswanderer-Schiff, Neapel', 'Emigrant-Ship, Naples'

(for Helga Hoffmeister)

One doesn't think of Rainer Maria Rilke (1875–1926) as writing poems on sociological or documentary themes, on subjects that might otherwise reside in newspapers and books of social history, anything like emigration or poverty or unemployment. Not much of the modern or contemporary world in Rilke of the Angels and the Contessas. Even in the context of unworldly poets, he is like one of those cabinet ministers who don't know the price of a bottle of milk. To some extent, one would be wrong. An early book of his was the so-called *Book of Hours*, with its sections 'On monastic life', 'On pilgrimage', and 'On poverty and death'. A slightly hallowed—haloed—version of poverty actually existed in him for a long time, albeit more as an adjunct to his romantic quasi-mediaevalism than as an interested reaction to the problems of industrialization or urbanization or mass-production. 'I sent you yesterday', he writes in a letter of October 1900, 'a little package of a very excellent oat cereal to try. Directions on the package. Only it is good to let it cook somewhat longer than the fifteen minutes prescribed. Before eating put a piece of butter in it, or take applesauce with it.... If you send for a patent "all-purpose" double boiler from a big household goods store, you hardly need to stir it; the danger of burning is very slight then.'[1] The letter, a culinary and cohabitational vote of no-confidence, is addressed to his wife of six months. (He is, in the terms he made famous, guarding her solitude.) His counsel is at once frugal and irredeemably fancy in its frugality, or frugalism, if you'll allow. Just the kind of thing one could imagine Baucis writing to her Philemon, if only they'd conducted their relationship by mail.

A much more serious text of poverty is Rilke's 1910 novel, *The Notebooks of Malte Laurids Brigge*, which sets Malte, his impoverished Danish aristocrat poet hero, in Paris, on a rapid downwardly mobile course. Malte reads in public libraries (he reads Ibsen), has trouble finding a place to eat, lives in solitude and squalor, joins Baudelaire in intoning the desperate, Pharisaical prayer of '*Une heure du matin*': 'grant me the grace to produce some fine verses'— some decent lines, I would say, *quelques beaux vers*—'that will prove to me that I am not the least of men, that I am not inferior to those I scorn'.[2] Rilke wrote at *Malte* for the best part of ten years. It conserves and expresses his initial shock at encountering Paris, abruptly falling out of a sort of fantasy feudalism as poetry's knight errant into the modern urban era. Rilke is associated with houses and towers and landscapes, not with cities, other than Paris. His places are watery Worpswede, the artists' colony outside Bremen, Russia, the Skane region of Sweden, the Egypt of the pyramids, Duino at the head of the Adriatic, the South of Spain and the Valais in the South of Switzerland that so magically reminds him of it. Nothing cramped or developed there. As he relates in a letter of July 1903 to Lou Andreas-Salome, it was quite as bad as what hitherto had been the worst nightmare of his life: 'I would like to tell you, dear Lou, that Paris was for me an experience similar to the military school; as a great fearful astonishment seized me then, so now again terror assailed me at everything that, as in an unspeakable confusion, is called life.'[3] One of his biographers, Ralph Freedman, says it in slang: 'Paris had been a bust.'[4] *Malte*, accordingly, was the hardest thing Rilke ever did—otherwise, writing came fatally easy to him. When it came out in 1910, he was a little aghast at what he had done, and he warned susceptible readers not to read it straight, but somehow 'against the grain'. The poems Rilke wrote at the same time were those that made up the *New Poems* of 1907 and 1908. Forget the horrid and ubiquitous *Letters to a Young Poet*, perplexed gift of mothers everywhere to their versifying juniors, forget *Duino*, forget the *Sonnets to Orpheus*. They are for me his greatest poems, and *Malte* his greatest book.[5]

The *New Poems* are written under the shadow of '*mon grand ami Auguste Rodin*' to whom their second (1908) volume was dedicated: Rilke had first gone to Paris in 1902, to write a monograph on Rodin (arranged by his sculptor wife, Clara Westhoff, who was a former pupil of Rodin's), and returned in 1905, to serve as the great man's secretary. The ground-note of all those years, probably strenuously denied by Rilke, is humiliation. (It's not that he couldn't 'do' reality, but only selectively, and only sometimes.) He was in his late twenties, like Malte, and unlike Malte, married, and not to the painter Paula Becker either. His years as a prodigy were behind him. Quaker Oats notwithstanding, he hadn't been able to keep his actual wife or feed their daughter, Ruth, who was left to eat 'alien corn' with her mother's parents; the most important person in his life, Lou Andreas-Salome, had ditched him after a brief and long-delayed erotic experiment, and confined herself thereafter to the giving of advice to her younger charge (yes, Rilke—himself the giver of so much advice, he seems to have entered the ranks of the writers of self-help books, or American wisdom literature, author of *Rilke on Love and Other Difficulties*, for those anxious to compound them, and numerous others—was told how to write his name and wear his hair); then the sage Tolstoy, while admitting Lou, had unforgettably snubbed him; Rodin humbled him with his all-too-visible, massive, unfussy production, it must have been like living in a hangar, with airplanes for company; so the role of his secretary—from which, further, he was dismissed 'like a dishonest servant'[6] in 1906, for taking too much initiative—can't have been easy for him. Paris, where he was straightforwardly re-classed as foreign and poor, will have been a continual humbling. Accordingly, *Malte* is full of extraordinary vignettes:

> Who are these people? What do they want from me? Are they waiting for me? How do they recognize me? It's true my beard looks somewhat neglected, and it is barely vaguely reminiscent of their sick, old, faded beards that always impressed me. But don't I have the right to neglect my beard? Many busy people do, and it would never occur to anyone to immediately lump them together with the outcasts on that account. For it is clear to me that these people are outcasts, not just beggars. No, they're really not beggars; one must discriminate. They are trash, husks of people spat out by fate. Damp from the saliva of fate they stick to a wall, to a lamppost, to an advertising pillar, or they slowly ooze down the street, leaving a dark, dirty trace behind. What in the world did that old woman want from me who, carrying the drawer of a night table in which a few buttons and needles were rolling around, had crept out of some hole or other? Why did she always walk beside me and look at me? As if she were trying to recognize me with her watery eyes that looked as if some sick person had spat green slime into her bleeding

lids? And how, that other time, did that small grey woman come to stand for a quarter of an hour beside me before a shop window while showing me an old, long pencil that protruded with infinite slowness from her filthy, closed hands? I acted as if I were looking at the goods displayed and didn't notice anything. But she knew I had seen her, she knew I was standing there and wondering what she was really doing. For I understood quite well that it could not be a question of the pencil: I felt that it was a sign, a sign for the initiated, a sign that the outcasts recognize; I felt she was indicating to me that I had to go somewhere or do something.[7]

Hence the gutter-level of his regard in *Malte*, the eyes literally or metaphorically cast down, locus of his quivering empathetic observation of the epileptic on the pavement, his queasy scanning of the life still sticking to the sides of torn-down houses, for the personal ordeal of the greasy back of the armchair in his rented room:

At first it was really hard for me to lay my head back in this armchair, for in its green covering there is a kind of smeary grey hollow into which all heads seem to fit. For quite a long time I took the precaution of putting a handkerchief behind my head, but now I'm too tired to; I have discovered that it works without it, and that the small indentation is made precisely for my head, as if to measure.[8]

Hence his most exalted dream, that of perhaps running a shop—and being able to afford to keep it closed to customers (a typically Rilkean proposition):

Sometimes I walk past small shops, perhaps in the rue de Seine. Dealers in antiques or engravings, or small antiquarian booksellers with overflowing display windows. No one ever goes in, it's obvious that they don't do any business. But if one looks inside they are sitting, sitting and reading, unconcerned; not worried about tomorrow, not anxious about success, have a dog sitting before them, happy, or a cat that makes the silence still larger as it slinks along the rows of books as if it were flicking the names off the spines.[9]

Which in the letter to Clara in which it was first formulated, goes on:

> Ah, if only this were enough: sometimes I dream of buying a full shop window like that and sitting down behind it with a dog for twenty years. In the evening there would be light in the back room, the front would be dark, and we would be sitting in back together, the three of us, eating; I've noticed how, when you look in from the street, it always looks like a Last Supper, so great and solemn through the dark room.[10]

It is a dream of non-being, of social and economic and biological inconsequence. Capitalism's shop window, without the shop. One might imagine the inside of an Egyptian tomb, with a few home comforts and a mummy of Bast or Mut in it. Instead, he walked straight into Baudelaire's old horror of the crowd, the *foule*, and to his own additional horror started rubbing shoulders with it. There is infinite downward mobility, in which the outrages received are matched only by one's capacity to feel them.

This *baisse* was something Rilke could only work his way out of. Otherwise there was only René Maria, the epicene son of Phia, the deserting husband, the absentee father, the menial employee, the émigré retained to write letters that a native could have written in a tenth of the time. He needed the torturous ten-year plan of *Malte*—to have failed at which might have left him at the bottom of a well—and if you like, the 'method' poems of the *Neue Gedichte*. Not waiting for inspiration, but taking the handicraft of a poem, and setting himself subjects, the way a shoemaker might, or a sculptor. Laocoon. The burghers of Calais. The thinker. The lovers. The tiny figurines and vast hands. And of course the other way around. 'The artist', writes Rilke in the monograph he wrote on Rodin in 1902:

> has the right to make one thing out of many and a world out of the smallest part of a thing. Rodin has made hands, independent, small hands which, without forming part of a body, are yet alive. Hands rising upright, angry and irritated, hands whose five bristling fingers seem to bark like the five throats of a Cerberus. Hands in motion, sleeping hands and hands in the act of awaking; criminal hands weighted by heredity, hands that are tired and have lost all desire, lying like some sick beast crouched in a corner, knowing none can help them.[11]

So Rilke took himself to the Paris zoo, called the Jardin des Plantes, where in living memory starving Communards had killed and eaten the elephant. He acquired an artist's pass and could visit during hours when it was closed to the public. He wrote 'The Panther', 'The Gazelle', 'The Flamingos'. He re-told stories from the Bible, and stories from antiquity. He documented his travels of those years. (He was fussy about place and places; his life's compass rose was marked by Russia and Spain, Sweden and Egypt. John Bayley called him the last European; I'd call him the last fusspot.) Artisanal work, work of the hands, he said later. Under Rodin's stamp, le modélé. 'Thing-poems', Dinggedichte, poems about things, but also poems that are 'a thing', not a mood or an atmosphere or a feeling, as too many of their predecessors had been. A few of them cast some of the Malte material as poems, Baudelairean encounters with unspeakable crones, the poor, beggars, lunatics. The mad, with the partitions taken out of their brains; the beggars, selling the inside of their hands; one of the old women, showing a patchwork smile under 'half a hat'. These are all glimpses, lifted from the *New Poems.* He took some of the humility of Rodin and his other great discovery of those years, Cézanne. He wrote, in October of 1907:

> You know how much more remarkable I always find the people walking about in front of paintings than the paintings themselves. It's no different in this Salon d'Automne, except for the Cézanne room. Here, all of reality is on his side: in this dense quilted blue of his, in his red and his shadowless green and the reddish black of his wine bottles. And the humbleness of all his objects: the apples are cooking apples and the wine bottles belong in the bulging pockets of an old coat.[12]

The two volumes of *New Poems* are, in my view, two of the most beautifully made poetic sequences ever. Even before he had finished the first part, in summer 1907, Rilke realized that one book would not be enough for the thing he was embarked on. The first volume appeared in December 1907; he wrote the second in a year and a day, from 31 July 1907 to 2 August 1908: ninety-nine poems. *New Poems (The Other Part)* was the last book of his own poems for fifteen years, before the late spate of the *Elegies* and *Sonnets.* The books have all the symmetries. They seem to be both reflected and rotated and pieced together. Poems suggest and follow each other; themes and words and constructions and preoccupations call out and resonate. It seems full of fractals. Distance does the work of adjacency, it barely matters in the crystalline structure. The blue hydrangea and the pink. The panther and the gazelle. Staircases and balconies. The cadet portrait of the father, and the self-portrait. Apollo to Apollo. Abishag to Abishag. Buddha to Buddha to Buddha. The Renaissance expressed now as Flanders, now as the Mediterranean. *New Poems (The Other Part)* begins with Apollo—you know the one—and ends with Buddha. It goes from the periphery to the centre, from the all-seeing perimeter of the archaic torso (one of very many sculptural subjects) to the 'center of all centers, core of cores', '*Mitte aller Mitten, Kern der Kerne*'.[13] From the injunction, 'You must change your life', to the changed life: 'Yet already there's begun inside you/ what lasts beyond the suns.'[14] And there, somewhere along the strung sequence of miracles, of mostly altered sonnets, mutated or truncated, and one of the least of them, is 'Emigrant-Ship (Naples)', following 'Easter Eve' and 'The Balcony' both also subtitled 'Naples'; and in advance of the Italian 'Landscape', a colour-study celebrating the blue hour, and 'Roman Campagna'. We have here a little locus, a little cluster of the sempiternal German love of Italy, from Alaric the Goth to Goethe, who eloped to Italy, not even telling his principality he was going; from the Emperor Henry IV who in 1077 went on his knees to Canossa to beg the forgiveness of Pope Gregory VII (it's entered the German language, to 'go to Canossa') to the eighteenth-century Johann Gottfried Seume, who walked to Syracuse; from Thomas Mann of *Death in Venice* to Wolfgang Koeppen of *Death in Rome*.

Rilke visited Naples several times, as a sort of staging-post, to or from Capri or Rome, in both of which he stayed for many months at a time. He was there for a few days in June of 1904, and again in November and December of 1906. He put up at the recently refurbished Hotel Hassler on the waterfront and seems to have experienced the typically mingled fortunes of visitors to the South: personal comfort and expense; geographical beauty in the distance and a certain amount of picturesque (and other) grime and misery at close quarters, when he went out. The hotel is slightly unusual as a setting for Rilke. He had little money and didn't like to spend it. More often, he stayed with people, as he did in Capri, or in their houses when they were gone, ideally leaving him their cooks and chauffeurs (as happened in Duino). The hotel makes him anonymous and vulnerable. No one knows who he is (as it says on his tombstone), and, worse, he is spending his own money. Naples, you might say, twinned with Paris. A big city, and what's more, a major port. This shear takes its toll on visitors, and it does so with Rilke. He keeps an eye out for what shifts, rather than what stays. 'The sea has already changed twenty times while I have been writing.'[15] From the boat, he watches Naples recede: 'it takes on more and more the character of an enormous quarry that is reddish and bright on its fresh surfaces between old, steep, long-unbroken grey. The deeper-lying parts finally fade away completely into reddish mist.' He thinks, as a tourist will, that he has come at the wrong time: 'Naples too, as indeed everything Italian, is more beautiful in the summer.'[16] His barber warns him of an impending change of weather: '*Pioggia, scirocco, eh*—.' He haunts the museum, takes refuge in his book he has brought with him from Munich: 'Title: Vincent Van Gogh, Letters....' He sees pictures, as he has been training himself to do. He writes about a fishmonger's stall, with so much death and nothing but death keeping him out ('suddenly you have the impression that you are standing in front of nothing but stone and metal, as you look across the table').[17] He tries himself out with colours (in those years he was learning form from Rodin, colour from Cézanne): 'I saw yesterday the stand of a lemonade seller. Posts, roof, and back of his little booth were blue (of that animated blue dulling toward green of certain Turkish and Persian amulets).'[18] He is patient, exposed, 'no one but you', he writes rather quodlibetically to his friends and patrons the von der Heydts, the dedicatees of the first volume of *New Poems*, 'knows what being completely alone, being unobserved, unseen, invisible means to me. For three days in Naples I went about with it as with a treasure in all the gloriously foreign world ....'[19]

The informal sequence of Naples poems has something of a little island of neo-Realism in Rilke. The 'Easter Eve' procession might have come from Rossellini's *Voyage to Italy*; 'The Balcony' from a cramped, multi-generational drama of Francisco Rosi's; 'Emigrant Ship' from the Taviani brothers' Pirandello adaptation, *Kaos*. All are street-level, seen in passing, with amateur actors. All have a photographic, documentary quality, not all that common in Rilke. It is as though he has brought his tourist's impressionability with him, along with his vulnerability from Paris. Again, unusually for Rilke, these are humble, even dingy poems, poems almost with a smell. In 'Easter Eve', the loaves stretching 'before the yawning of the melons', the dead and condemned beasts voluptuous in death, the perishable, anxiety-inducing, flyblown plenty of the South, the ox, the goats, the lambs, the roosters, till the—unexpected and utterly cinematic—show-stealing monkey shows up at the finish, perhaps something puncturing to Easter, or to Christ, or the poet. A riotous poem, somehow, like something by Levi-Strauss. Rilke wasn't in Naples in Easter, or at least not in 1906; these 'New Poems' were written later, or dated later, to summer 1908.

Then 'The Balcony',[20] a favourite subject of the poet's, often given an aristocratic elevation, though not here, where the reader can readily imagine generations in black. (On the same day, though, 17 August 1907, he wrote 'Lady on the Balcony', also in the *New Poems*, in its own proper context of lady-poems.) Often too, though, the balcony offers the outlook looked back at, the watchers watched, the bunched faces looked up at and made something of. Manet's 'The Balcony' has been mentioned as a possible source for the poem, but it could just as well be personal impression or a photograph. It seems to hark back to the more famous and personal poems, 'Self-Portrait 1906' and 'Cadet Portrait of my Father' (who had died that same year). The subject might be 'live', might be a photograph: part of the stock in trade of these poems is the way they confer animation or rigidity upon what they behold. The form is a little interesting, the first stanza, six lines, one sentence; the next five, nineteen lines, the second sentence. The balcony pulls the people together, seems to bunch their faces into a 'bouquet'. Two sisters, a brother, their mother, an even older woman, and a single child. A family without a single couple, long-lived and short-lifed, so to speak; the brevity in the South of attraction and vigour. Perhaps here too Rilke is thinking of his mother, now a widow, who was to outlive her son, his father deceased the previous year, his absent wife, his child, an etiolated line. The balcony hangs like a balloon, or a bunch of balloons, as the faces and the generations float away into indeterminacy—there's the echo of the 'Self-Portrait 1906'—'wie noch unbestimmbar, wie noch nicht' (as if still undefinable, still deferred), and sometimes, furthermore, crossed out by the bars, like the panther which padded along to inaugurate the beginning of this sequence of 'New Poems', back in 1902 or 1903.

The holiday swarm and plenty; then the watchers and the wreckage of family; finally, the ones who are doing what Rilke seems to prescribe at the outset, in the 'Archaic Torso', changing their lives: the emigrants. 'Emigrant-Ship' is actually Rilke's second take at both subject and title; there was an earlier, unrelated treatment from 1894, when he was all of 18. He wrote it in Bohemia—a strange thing for a piece, set, as it were, in Illyria. 'The spark for the aberrant verses', writes George Schoolfield in *Young Rilke and His Time*, 'can only be guessed at'.[21] It was written in irregular verse, and then re-cast in the modish prose-poem mode, with the same excitable dot-dot-dot punctuation. In either guise, it cuts with offensive speed from distance-shot to close-up. The ship barely exists as a knocked-together frame for the standard terrified *fin de siecle* portrait of feminine desire.[22]

What the teenage Rilke wrote, apparently in full seriousness and with heavy reliance on expectable adjectives, was this (slightly compressed):

> Emigrant-ship. Packed to the gunwales. Well-to-do, laughing, strolling, feasting. Deep below in fume-filled cabins, where only the cheerless lamp burns with a tired light, the poor. Men, women. Pale, sullen, pressed tight together by uncertain fear. Dulled faces, stupefied, careworn…*One* woman though…Pale and still with large eyes, tear-laden, deeply dark; with eyes that solicit passionate love, solicit so greedily. Sallow lips that quiver as though from tears choked back, golden-brown hair in locks half undone shadowing her forehead. […] And once again her eyes.—As though for this life's secret they sought the grave solution…Will they ever find it?—There?—I do not know. Only sometimes in sleepless nights do these eyes rise up before me…yes, these tired eyes, athirst for death …. [23]

It seems unlikely that this woman is travelling below decks, though we're not told; Schoolfield dubs her 'an advance member of Rene's rich gallery of women variously beset'.[24] A recent widow? Pregnant? A murderess? All are possible; Rilke has yet to master the convincing scene-from-a-novel type of poem he knocked out so brilliantly later, like 'Before Summer Rain' or 'The Shako' or 'Piano Practice'. The piece is called 'Fantasy' and subtitled 'a poem in prose'. Enough already.

The second 'Emigrant-Ship' is both immediate—we see the striking 'Naples' and believe—and at the same time strangely distanced, distanced into colour, into (like many of the new poems) geometry or a sort of history of energy—think Cézanne, then think Rodin—and into a rather difficult meaning. I'll give it to you first in Edward Snow's literal English version:[25]

Emigrant-Ship
Naples

Imagine: that someone fled hot and burning,
and the victors were close behind,
and all at once the fleeing one turned,
abrupt, unexpected, and charged
against hundreds—: that intensely
the glow of all the fruit threw itself
again and again at the blue sea:

as the slow-moving orange boat
carried them past, on out to the huge
gray ship, into which, from thrust to thrust,
other boats were lifting fish, bread,—
while it, full of scorn, took
coal into its womb, open like death.

Now in J.B. Leishman's 'form-identical' version, and you will see how imperilled this kind of thing is, and maybe understand why a lot of these 'New Poems' remain unknown:

Think: that one were fleeing, hot and glowing,
with the victors gaining rapidly,
and the fleer suddenly
turned and hurtled unexpectedly
upon hundreds:—so impetuously
did the glow of fruits there keep on throwing
its reflection in the dark blue sea

18

as the orange-boat would slowly press
over with them to the shortly-leaving
great, grey ship, where other boats were heaving
fish and bread up with such willingness,
while it, full of scorn, went on receiving
coal into its death-wide openness.[26]

And in the original:

Auswanderer-Schiff
(*Neapel*)

Denk: daß einer heiß und glühend flüchte,
und die Sieger wären hinterher,
und auf einmal machte der
Flüchtende kurz, unerwartet, Kehr
gegen Hunderte—: so sehr
warf sich das Erglühende der Früchte
immer wieder an das blaue Meer:

als das langsame Orangen-Boot
sie vorübertrug bis an das große
graue Schiff, zu dem, von Stoß zu Stoße,
andre Boote Fische hoben, Brot,—
während es, voll Hohn, in seinem Schooße
Kohlen aufnahm, offen wie der Tod.

'*Denk*', it begins, 'think' or 'imagine', in the imperative. ('*Denk es wäre nicht*', begins another one of the New Poems called 'Gold', 'imagine that it weren't', where we are asked to believe or conceive the gold, as elsewhere we are asked to believe or conceive the unicorn. The impossible is Rilke's terrain, and the conditional or subjunctive his mood. Think: '*Wer, wenn ich schriee, hörte mich denn*', or '*So, also hierher kommen die Leute, um zu leben, ich würde eher meinen, es stürbe sich hier*' to give two prominent examples, the very beginning of the *Elegies*, and of *Malte*. Here it is '*flüchte*'.) The poem 'Emigrant-Ship' is a metaphor that almost capsizes it. Someone is running away, fleeing for his life, pursued by enemies. Our emigrant, we suppose, initially, or a whole ship of them. Wrong, but carry on anyway. Suddenly he turns, and makes bold to confront his enemies, but it turns out he is just a personification, a measure of intensity, for another rhetorical figure, a visual metaphor, for a boat full of oranges that insistently and repeatedly goes out into the blue bay. See Naples, you recall, and die. The visible is both heightened and almost annulled by the metaphor. Number, as it often is for Rilke, who thought he should be allowed to use a cardinal plural with a singular noun, as in 'Two Evening', is a problem. Can a boatful of oranges coming and going be likened to a single warrior? At a pinch. Big pinch of pink Himalayan salt. Meanwhile—sestet now—while the orange boat is going out, other boats are going too, and going faster, and seemingly more purposefully, loading bread and fish— we think of the biblical miracle of their multiplication, we can't help ourselves—into a grey ship, all the while the ship itself is being loaded, with coals.

We see blue and orange and grey and (the unstated) black. Or blue, then orange, then grey, then black. The livelier colours give way. They are puddled together to make grey. Something is being seen here, has been seen here, but it gives way to a point of view. It is a strangely coercive poem. There is something gallant about the oranges, they are going to their doom, they are heroic, they remind one of the Greeks at Thermopylae—the hot gates—successively, individually halting the Persian advance. Just as much as a darkening and a dulling, the poem enacts a cooling, a loss of vital energies. Then the fish and the bread, no colour, less glamorous, the unavoidable echo of scripture—almost polluted, and certainly dwarfed by the ship's greater need, for coal. Full of scorn—why scorn? What is being scorned here? Is it the simultaneous or successive appetites? One might have expected 'Hohn', 'scorn', to be a stand-by in Rilke, a useful way of bringing in a far-fetched comparison, or contrast, or simultaneity, every bit as frequent as such other regular standbys of his as 'until' or 'however' or 'suddenly'—actually it seems to be rather rare, and only to occur in a few early biblical poems. We seem to see a diagram, simple arrows going through the blue, out to the grey ship's cavernous open hold: first orange, then black. Imagine something like a Paul Klee painting. So many of the *New Poems* resolve themselves to an account of energy, something almost like a preposition. They are like illustrations of the idea of 'through' or 'into' or 'around' or 'up'. They are redistributive, ontologically (though not politically) rebellious: the archaic torso that sees you; the cadaver giving orders in a room; the recovering invalid stroking her bony chin. But think of Klee. Here there is an orange line, going first one way (fleeing), then another, thicker, fighting back, confronting the blue; then the black, heavily scratched over the orange. Towards a grey rectangle. We had something pretty for a while, but it was obliterated. The fire cools to coal. Most generously, an existing life, a furnished life, a life in progress (orange, warm, maybe Europe, hand-made) reverts to one in potential (black, cold, maybe America, mechanical).

We have successively something like a picture (the pretty contrast of orange and blue), then a meaning (orange and black across blue, into grey: a ship is being loaded up), then an attitude. The poem doesn't see the unanimous columns of émigrés, the caravan of departing souls, the bravery and drama of their wager, their confrontation of the impossible, their changing their lives. Where is their real heroism, their actual resistance? These are just oranges bobbing out to sea—Greeks being swallowed up by Persians. They are kowtowing. Perhaps then at the latest we notice there are no actual people in the poem at all. A human subject with no humans. We are just told a story in terms of colour, in objects, and in expectations. Something told evidentially, but impersonally. In a kind of reading of an image. The rhymes compete—the feminine triad is *eros*, '*grosse*', '*stosse*', '*schoosse*'; 'great', 'thrusts' (in admittedly another sense of '*stosse*', here it means something more like 'pallets'), 'womb'—and the masculine *thanatos*, '*Boot*', '*Brot*', '*Tod*'; boat, bread, death. Rhymes where they are used often give one a rudimentary, accelerated sense of where a poem is going. So here: boat—bread—death. The poem bears an odd resemblance to 'Orpheus. Eurydice. Hermes'—a movement heading towards light and colour, before abruptly the destination changes, and we are told it is death. (The way Rilke tells it, remember, it is not a sad story.) The single warrior of Thermopylae is Eurydice. She flees to life, then turns to die. It's splendid. 'Who?' she says, when told her husband Orpheus has turned to look at her, thus breaking their compact. 'Who?' says Rilke too. People leaving, poor people emigrating are implicitly likened to coals rumbling into an empty hold, to be burned. Wikipedia tells us that between 1860 and World War I, a staggering nine million Italians left permanently of a total of sixteen million who emigrated, most from the South and most to North or South America. Between 1901 and 1915, annual emigration averaged almost 600,000.[27]

The vilification and spite of the Italian in his (as R.B. Cunninghame-Graham wrote) 'greasy velveteen suit' is not Rilke's style, and his thought is not for the pristine land and people yonder, in which he took no interest, in which in some sense he did not even believe. Is that really what they've signed on for? And is that Rilke's take on emigration—scorn—or on the 'huddled masses', here, during these peak years of Italian emigration? The promised land, heaven on earth, the people's otherworld of justice, as Les Murray writes, the last best hope of mankind—why shouldn't one have to die to reach it? The Rilke scholar Eudo Mason writes, on *Malte*, but it is as applicable here: 'Rilke is not driven by indignation at the injustice of society, nor even, at least not principally, by human sympathy, but by absolute horror.' What he sees here is a mass phenomenon, bulk provisioning, as literal as you like, the crowd taking ship to be a crowd somewhere else. As the poet himself wrote about *Malte*, his task was 'to make things from fear', '*Dinge machen aus Angst*'. The 'heat' and 'glow' of the opening dims to a cold death. The account of a real event or situation follows instead a Rilke-preset: the thirst for death evinced in so many of the poems in the *Neue Gedichte*— and that was already present in the early 'Fantasy', '*todesdurstig*', 'athirst for death'. The mass-destiny elicits a predictable failure of compassion from Rilke (it's true, he doesn't like plurals, and as Mason observes, he didn't have the least sympathy for revolutionary, egalitarian, or socialist endeavours), watching from his ringside seat in Hassler's Hotel (five stars, made over in the 1880s to the no-doubt superior management of the family of Swiss hoteliers) at the drama of hundreds of thousands of departing Italians, who—as we are told—left principally the countryside (Naples the one urban exception) in their droves, but are here invisible, clutching or embodying the warmth of their native oranges, their faith in loaves and fishes (nothing about the starvation offered them at home), but have accepted willingly or unwittingly their function as a raw material loaded into a vast and rapacious economy. The sort of technical, collective, and futuristic vision that Rilke didn't like to be exposed to. The sort of unconditional tenderness and participation and curiosity that Rilke didn't have, though Chekhov, travelling at about the same sort of time in Siberia, did:

> These migrants, who are footing it along the road behind their carts, are silent. Their faces have a serious, concentrated look. I watch them and reflect that it requires heroic strength of character to pull up stakes and say goodbye to a home, a region, a familiar way of life.[28]

Even when offered such a scene outside, it would seem, his hotel window, Rilke refuses it. It violates his creed of the passivity and singularity of life.

The drama of the single man, '*der Flüchtende*', is among the most perverse of Rilke's unlikely similes. He has turned the vast, optimistic-to-desperate social movement of hundreds of thousands over decades into a heroic and quixotic spur-of-the-moment individual impulse seeking its certain doom! He approves the latter; on the former he has nothing to say. Egon Schwarz writes: 'Rilke's abhorrence of machines, of everything that has to do with technology and mechanics, is no less well known than his dread of the city.'[29] Machines are among the stranger presences in the *Sonnets to Orpheus*, and it's true, they get a very bad press. II 10 begins, '*Alles Erworbne bedroht die Maschine*', 'All we have gained the machine threatens', in Stephen Mitchell's translation. In # 2 of the Appendix to the Sonnets, sounding much more like the preachy crank he sometimes thinks he is, Rilke writes: '*O das Neue, Freunde, ist nicht dies,/ dass Maschinen uns die Hand verdrängen./ Lasst euch nicht beirrn von Übergängen,/ bald wird schweigen, wer das "Neue" pries.*' 'The New, my friends, is not a matter of/ letting machines force out our handiwork./ Don't be confused by change; soon those who have/ praised the "New" will realize their mistake.' The emigrant-ship here is grey, like a battleship, '*das grosse,/ graue Schiff*'. In an aestheticizing poem, it registers almost as an absence. It has zero aesthetic appeal; in terms of aesthetic value, '*gross*' is about where '*grau*' is. In Rilke's lexicon, ships have nothing of the prettiness or the subtle eroticism they have in Joseph Roth, where they are habitually described as 'bridal-white'. There is an ecstatic harbour-scene of Odessa in Roth's 'Leviathan' that goes:

> Wherever he looks, he sees nothing but ships and water, water and ships. There are the ships, the boats, the tugs, the yachts, the motorboats apple blossom white, raven black, coral red, yes, coral red—and there is the water washing against their sides, no, not washing but lapping and stroking, in thousands of little wavelets, like tongues and hands at once.[30]

This maybe corresponds to the erotic side of the rhymes in Rilke's sestet. But then the surprising, dismaying ending, '*offen wie der Tod*', 'open as death', takes one back to the dead dolphin at the end of 'Birth of Venus' in the 1907 *New Poems*: '*tot, rot und offen*', 'dead, red and open' or perhaps 'slashed, red and dead'. Rilke seems not only to be describing something he doesn't understand—one might say it is only the mention of death that brings it closer to him— and something he would never personally contemplate (the distance between Hassler's Hotel and the unnamed ship is, one might say, unbridgeable), but even to be doing it anachronistically, from the unhelpful vantage point of some earlier century.[31] His orientation has retreated into its feudal base, his poetic imagination is at its most abstract, and it sees something merely ghastly. He is a spectator, like the well-situated guest at a Roman circus, watching the gladiators. He gives it the thumbs-down. The world is like that of some science fiction, when the needs and abilities of machines have outstripped those of foolish, desperate humans. Hence perhaps '*Hohn*', 'scorn'. Perhaps it is like Fritz Lang's *Metropolis*, a film released in 1926, the year Rilke died: the steam-punk vision of the half-timbered Tudor cottage, the pretty girl, and the vast anonymous and anonymizing processes of proletarian labour.

At the end of his life, in a series of letters to his Polish translator, Witold von Hulewicz, Rilke writes about the descent of man and of man-made things:

> the ever more rapid fading away of so much of the visible that will no longer be replaced. Even for our grandparents a 'house', a 'well', a familiar tower, their very clothes, their coat: were infinitely more, infinitely more intimate; almost everything a vessel in which they found the human and added to the store of the human. Now, from America, empty indifferent things are pouring across, sham things, dummy life ... . A house, in the American sense, an American apple or a grapevine over there, has nothing in common with the house, the fruit, the grape into which went the hopes and reflections of our forefathers ... . Live things, things lived and conscient of us, are running out and can no longer be replaced. We are perhaps the last still to have known such things.[32]

A 'vessel', he says; this other vessel and its mission are not to his liking. The unmanned and denatured things from America, the 'American apple and the grapevine over there' were and continued to be a trope about America. (It is at the root of the old jeer about Californian wine, 'the grapes haven't suffered enough'; while Hans Magnus Enzensberger has drily described the USA as a place where bread has been successfully rendered extinct.) It is there in the Hollywood poems of Brecht, who did get there, forty years later: 'And fruit markets/ With great heaps of fruit, albeit having/ Neither smell nor taste',[33] and on into Adorno and the 'simulacra' of Baudrillard. Evelyn Juers begins her dazzling book on Heinrich Mann and the California exiles with a little flutter of fictional excitement: gooseberries have been sighted in Santa Monica. In

Rilke, the oranges are going—gaily, gallantly—to their death; his emigrant-ship is a death-ship; his poem is an exequy. Rilke is right out of sympathy with the scale of what he is describing, the medium of it, and the purpose of it. The idea of a class or even a whole population taking ship to better itself, or even to survive at all will have been disagreeable to him, with his promotion of passivity and his feudal and static playing-card version of society from king to beggar (note: all singulars, no more than one of each). It wasn't in him to see desperate emigrants as versions of himself, or the poet—except in *Malte*—as socially imprinted or configured at all, downwardly mobile in society and doomed in economics. Less comically than in the early prose-poem but just as determinedly, he refuses even to see what was put in front of him. Instead, he substitutes an individual action from the heroic age, a little by-play of colour, faith, and flavour—oranges, fish, bread, blue—and his preferred *terminus ad quem*, death. The poem seems doomy, Mediterranean, death-bound. An Alcestis by other means (Alcestis, who chose to die on behalf of her husband Admetus, is a sensible heroine to Rilke, just as Eurydice was). *Boot-Brot-Tod*. The emigrants in their black suits and widows' weeds— crepe and corduroy—going to die abroad. With, perhaps most unforgivably, hope in their hearts. And nothing rhymes with orange. Dying abroad, the idea provoked an almost Greek horror in Rilke. When the actress and *tragédienne* Eleonora Dusa died at the Schenley Hotel in Pittsburgh on 21 April 1924, Rilke wrote to one of his duchesses[34]: '*Eleonora Duse est morte, morte loin de nous, dans un pays—on voudrait presque dire dans un monde étranger.... Quelle tristesse*' ('Eleonora Dusa is dead, dead far from us, in a foreign land—one would almost say in a foreign world.... What sadness').

And then, the following day, to one of his intimates, Nanny Wunderly-Volkart: '*La mort de la Duse! Et encore en Amerique, a Pittsbourg, en pays étranger, non, il faudrait dire dans un autre monde; elle, qui aimait tant etre soutenue par son entourage, de mourir en Amerique, dans un hotel de Pittsbourg—; Dieu sait si quelqu'un coeur ami était au pres d'elle!*' ('The death of the Duse! And, worse, in America, in Pittsburgh, in a foreign land, no, in almost another world; she, who so depended on the support of her entourage, dying in America, in a hotel in Pittsburgh—God knows if she had a friendly heart by her anywhere!') America is where art, reality, and individuality go to die. 'Many of Rodin's works have gone to America', he writes, 'the finest being destroyed in the Chilean disturbances before ever it was placed in position',[35] the two halves of the sentence balancing as though they meant one and the same thing: 'have gone to America' and 'being destroyed'.

Ironically—and this is one place where one might reach for the word *Hohn*—I've sometimes described Rilke as an American poet. America has bought the world of interiority, spirituality, angels. Of effusions and euphemisms and euphuisms. Having claimed the lion's share of this world, it is reserving the next. Most things are decisively transformed by having an 'American' planted in front of them: American Beauty, American sonnet, American angst, American alliteration. Rilke, to me, would sit very nicely there, 'in any number of "new age" and consciousness exploring contexts', as one critic says,[36] in a sort of garbled literary Disneyworld. It's almost at hand, so that one almost doesn't need to imagine, using the cutting words of Egon Schwarz, 'the enormous metaphorical edifice of the Prague prophet...something of a Taj Mahal of poetry that stands functionless in its environment, gaped at uncomprehendingly by the curious'.[37] It was the shrewd German novelist Annette Kolb who first saw Rilke making millions on the American lecture circuit.[38] So let's imagine him like that, in a Rilkean spirit of counter-factualism, taken out of the coal-hole and orange again, having done well for himself on bread and fish, pretending to disregard but actually directing the sum of misconceptions about him that (as he himself said) constitutes a reputation, mingling with the Celtic showmen Oscar Wilde and Dylan Thomas, with Dickens of the spittoons and Trollope of the politicians, with the temporary Auden and the still more temporary MacNeice, with the missile makers in New Mexico and the clever German Jewish Left clustered unhappily around Hollywood, retailing the old world and its soft wisdom to the new. When the War ends, he is still not quite 70.

2

ARTHUR RIMBAUD

'Le Bateau Ivre', 'The Drunken Ship'

It's exactly one hundred lines, *pace* Edmund White, who unaccountably says it's twice that.[1] Not punishment (though perhaps calling out for it) but a wild form of demonstration or display or appeal for extra credit. It was written exactly a hundred and fifty years ago, in 1871, in the author's home town of Charleville near the Belgian frontier, on the River Meuse, where the author, who liked to play in boats but had never seen the sea,[2] was 16 and a schoolboy. Twenty-five quatrains of rhyming alexandrines—the classic French verse form of Racine and Du Bellay, the twelve-syllable line with the caesura metronomically after six—describing prophetically, cosmically, historically, culturally, the author's unconfined abandon, dissolution, quest for adventure, regress. A poem that is an autobiography, a prophecy, a promissory note, a goodbye. Rimbaud's wonderful biographer, Graham Robb, pictures the scene:[3]

> On the eve of his great departure, he went for a walk with Delahaye. It was a sunny autumn afternoon. They sat down at the edge of a wood and Rimbaud pulled out some sheets of paper. He had written a 100-line poem 'to show the people in Paris'. The verse was quite regular, but the content was extraordinary. Abruptly, without any rhetorical introduction, a boat recounted its adventures since the massacre of its crew—its astounding visions and gradual disintegration.

Then it was put in the post and mailed to Paul Verlaine. A sea-log
in exchange for the single train-ticket Verlaine sent him. A calling-
card of sorts. To show the people in Paris.

In 1871, the time of writing, Charles Baudelaire—the author of
poems with such apposite titles as 'L'Albatros', 'Le Voyage', and 'Le
Beau Navire'—had been dead for four years. Victor Hugo was liv-
ing in exile on Guernsey, which he made to seem like a savage
place. Edgar Allan Poe had written Arthur Gordon Pym, or maybe
vice versa. The world was full of things a schoolboy might have
read or heard about, never mind an advanced schoolboy like
Rimbaud, with an advanced library habit: Dumas, Verne, Melville,
Dana. The Suez Canal, ten years in the digging, was opened in
1869. The map of the world was patched like Sam Pig's trousers, of
course in pink, but also in blue (this is called Francophonie, and is
to some extent a continuing project). Its white—in the sense of
unknown—patches were dwindling. Most of its territories were
spoken for, or about to be, as late entrants to the colonial dash
appeared in Belgium and Germany, claiming, they too, their places
in the sun. That same year, Henry Morton Stanley ran into the
missing missionary David Livingstone, who had disappeared five
years previously. Dr Livingstone, I presume. Stanley went on to
search for the source of the Nile and explore the Congo and claim
its territory for the Belgian Leopold. If you see Herzog's Fitzcarraldo
or read Heart of Darkness about Marlow's arrival at his new place of
work, you will get the idea. It was a period of magical geography.
The world was somehow growing and shrinking at the same time.
Colonialism, emigration, exploration, religious missions, all were
a draw away from the 'ramparts of Europe'. The populations of
Ireland and Scandinavia and the newly unified Italy and Germany
seemed to be draining away. Jews were fleeing pogroms in Eastern

Europe. As for the technology, rails were being laid everywhere and counter-intuitive metal ships had been in existence since the 1840s. The iron-clad Monitor class of battleship was launched in 1862 and saw action—for both sides—in the American Civil War. At the same time, sailing-ships continued to be refined and quickened throughout the 1850s and 1860s. Joseph Conrad's maritime career comprised both. 'Voile et vapeur'—sail and steam— is the French formulation. It is also slang for bisexual, which is something our poet would shortly learn something about.

It's not enough, of course, but it's a start. A poem isn't a poem unless it's more than the sum of its parts. And then one might throw in Joseph Brodsky's *mot* about why we have the twentieth century when we've already had the nineteenth. Because this is a poem that rolls backwards and forwards. We see Rimbaud twenty years later, dying in Marseille; then, fast backwards, having his right leg taken off for cancer; limping ashore under protest; being put on a boat in Aden; being carried across the desert on a litter for twelve agonizing days; living for years as 'Abdoh Rinbo', a trader (camels, hides, coffee, small arms) and explorer in North East Africa; working with a travelling circus in Denmark and Sweden; deserting from the Dutch Colonial Army; joining same. It is hard not to think that Rimbaud ditched the adventure of literature for adventure *tout court*. Think Harrison Ford as Indiana Jones or Richard Chamberlain in *King Solomon's Mines*. As such, 'Le Bateau Ivre' is one of the last of his indirectnesses. A poem that seems to have as much of its business with the future as the past, and as much in the future of other literatures as in the future of its author.[4] Chief among its inheritors or beneficiaries was Bertolt Brecht. Among its English translators were Beckett and Lowell, Alan Jenkins and John Hartley Williams. Some dozen German translations have been made since K.L. Ammer's initial attempt appeared in 1908. Notable versions include those by the Expressionist Theodor Däubler (not a bad shot, in wild rhyming fourteeners)[5] and Paul Celan (in alexandrines, complete with the 'classic caesura').

Le Bateau ivre

Comme je descendais des Fleuves impassibles
Je ne me sentis plus guidé par les haleurs:
Des Peaux-rouges criards les avaient pris pour cibles
Les ayant cloués nus aux poteaux de couleurs.

J'étais insoucieux de tous les équipages,
Porteur de blés flamands ou de cotons anglais.
Quand avec mes haleurs ont fini ces tapages
Les Fleuves m'ont laissé descendre où je voulais.

Dans les clapotements furieux des marées,
Moi, l'autre hiver, plus sourd que les cerveaux d'enfants,
Je courus! Et les Péninsules démarrées
N'ont pas subi tohu-bohus plus triomphants.

La tempête a béni mes éveils maritimes.
Plus léger qu'un bouchon j'ai dansé sur les flots
Qu'on appelle rouleurs éternels de victimes,
Dix nuits, sans regretter l'œil niais des falots!

Plus douce qu'aux enfants la chair des pommes sures,
L'eau verte pénétra ma coque de sapin
Et des taches de vins bleus et des vomissures
Me lava, dispersant gouvernail et grappin.

Et dès lors, je me suis baigné dans le Poème
De la Mer, infusé d'astres, et lactescent,
Dévorant les azurs verts; où, flottaison blême
Et ravie, un noyé pensif parfois descend;

Où, teignant tout à coup les bleuités, délires
Et rhythmes lents sous les rutilements du jour,
Plus fortes que l'alcool, plus vastes que nos lyres,
Fermentent les rousseurs amères de l'amour!

Je sais les cieux crevant en éclairs, et les trombes
Et les ressacs et les courants: je sais le soir,
L'aube exaltée ainsi qu'un peuple de colombes
Et j'ai vu quelquefois ce que l'homme a cru voir!

J'ai vu le soleil bas, taché d'horreurs mystiques,
Illuminant de longs figements violets,
Pareils à des acteurs de drames très-antiques
Les flots roulant au loin leurs frissons de volets!

J'ai rêvé la nuit verte aux neiges éblouies,
Baiser montant aux yeux des mers avec lenteurs,
La circulation des sèves inouïes,
Et l'éveil jaune et bleu des phosphores chanteurs!

J'ai suivi, des mois pleins, pareille aux vacheries
Hystériques, la houle à l'assaut des récifs,
Sans songer que les pieds lumineux des Maries
Pussent forcer le mufle aux Oceans poussifs!

J'ai heurté, savez-vous, d'incroyables Florides
Mêlant aux fleurs des yeux de panthères a peaux
D'hommes! Des arcs-en-ciel tendus comme des brides
Sous l'horizon des mers, à de glauques troupeaux!

J'ai vu fermenter les marais énormes, nasses
Où pourrit dans les joncs tout un Léviathan!
Des écroulements d'eaux au milieu des bonaces
Et les lointains vers les gouffres cataractant!

Glaciers, soleils d'argent, flots nacreux, cieux de braises!
Echouages hideux au fond des golfes bruns
Où les serpents géants dévorés des punaises
Choient, des arbres tordus, avec de noirs parfums!

J'aurais voulu montrer aux enfants ces dorades
Du flot bleu, ces poissons d'or, ces poissons chantants.
—Des écumes de fleurs ont bercé mes dérades
Et d'ineffables vents m'ont ailé par instants.

Parfois, martyr lassé des pôles et des zones,
La mer dont le sanglot faisait mon roulis doux
Montait vers moi ses fleurs d'ombre aux ventouses jaunes
Et je restais, ainsi qu'une femme à genoux...

Presque île, ballottant sur mes bords les querelles
Et les fientes d'oiseaux clabaudeurs aux yeux blonds,
Et je voguais, lorsqu'à travers mes liens frêles
Des noyés descendaient dormir, à reculons!

Or moi, bateau perdu sous les cheveux des anses,
Jeté par l'ouragan dans l'éther sans oiseau,
Moi dont les Monitors et les voiliers des Hanses
N'auraient pas repêché la carcasse ivre d'eau;

Libre, fumant, monté de brumes violettes,
Moi qui trouais le ciel rougeoyant comme un mur,
Qui porte, confiture exquise aux bons poètes,
Des lichens de soleil et des morves d'azur,

Qui courais, taché de lunules électriques,
Planche folle, escorté des hippocampes noirs,
Quand les juillets faisaient crouler à coups de triques
Les cieux ultramarins aux ardents entonnoirs;

Moi qui tremblais, sentant geindre à cinquante lieues
Le rut des Béhémots et les Maelstroms épais,
Fileur éternel des immobilités bleues,
Je regrette l'Europe aux anciens parapets!

J'ai vu des archipels sidéraux! et des îles
Dont les cieux délirants sont ouverts au vogueur:
Est-ce en ces nuits sans fonds que tu dors et t'exiles,
Million d'oiseaux d'or, ô future Vigueur?—

Mais vrai, j'ai trop pleuré! Les Aubes sont navrantes.
Toute lune est atroce et tout soleil amer:
L'âcre amour m'a gonflé de torpeurs enivrantes.
O que ma quille éclate! O que j'aille à la mer!

Si je désire une eau d'Europe, c'est la flache
Noire et froide où vers le crépuscule embaumé
Un enfant accroupi plein de tristesses, lâche
Un bateau frêle comme un papillon de mai.

Je ne puis plus, baigné de vos langueurs, ô lames,
Enlever leur sillage aux porteurs de cotons,
Ni traverser l'orgueil des drapeaux et des flammes,
Ni nager sous les yeux horribles des pontons.

Jeremy Harding's translation

Drunken Boat

On my way down inscrutable Rivers
My haulers seemed to slacken off the ropes—
Yelping redskins had taken good aim,
Stripped them and nailed them to painted poles.

The crews and cargo meant nothing to me
—Flemish wheat or English cottons.
The clamour was done with, and so were the haulers.
The Rivers took me downstream as I pleased.

A winter ago, fast like a child in its own head,
I ran with the wild lapping
Of the tide-rips. Drifting peninsulas
Were never prey to such formidable commotion!

My awakenings at sea were graced by storms.
Lighter than a cork, I danced on the waves—
Eternal breakers of men, some say. Ten nights
Without the imbecile blink of harbour beacons.

Sweeter than flesh of sour apples to a child,
Green water surged through my pine-plank hull,

Washing out the stains of vomit and bluish wine—
It bore off my rudder, and my grapnel too.

From that time on, I basked in the Poem of the Sea,
A milk-white suspension of stars that devours
Raw azures. Through it drowned men
Fall like bleached driftwood, heavy with trance.

In that Poem, slow deliriums in shifting light
—Stronger than liquor, more enormous than lyres—
Infiltrate the bluenesses with bitter, drastically
Fermented rednesses of love.

I know skies fissured by lightning, water-spouts,
Breakers, undertows. I know dusk
And dawn, rising like a multitude of doves.
What men have only thought they'd seen, I've seen.

I've seen the low sun, flecked with mystic horrors,
Cast its monumental, violet welts of light,
Like figures in an antique drama,
On the distant, louvred surface of the rolling sea.

In the green night, I dreamed of snow-dazzle,
A slow kiss rising to the eyes of the ocean,
The circulation of bizarre sap,
Siren phosphorus, dawning blue and yellow.

For months at a stretch I've pursued the swells
That stampede on the reefs like maddened steer.
I never did believe in Marys-of-the-Sea who stifle
Wheezing oceans with their shining feet.

I've struck amazing Floridas, you know.
In the thick of their flora, panther eyes stare
From the hides of men. Rainbows crouch harness-taut
On glaucous wave-herds under the horizon of the seas.

I've seen vast, seething swamps, fish traps
In the rushes where entire Leviathans fester;

Downpours of water in the midst of calm;
Perspective hurtling over the abyss;

Glaciers, silver suns, reaches like mother-of-pearl, furnace skies!
Hideous wrecks at the bottom of deep, brown sumps
Where gigantic snakes, maddened by vermin and stinking
Of blackness, plummet from twisted trees.

I might have shown children the dorados
In the blue waters—and golden fish, and fish that sing.
Flower-strewn foam rocked me adrift
And ineffable winds supplied me with wings.

Sometimes I grew tired—a martyr of the latitudes and poles—
Then the sobbing ocean rolled me gently,
Made me offerings of shadow-flowers with yellow suckers,
And I hung there, like a kneeling woman.

I had become a floating island; the shit and bickerings
Of rowdy, pale-eyed birds slid down my flanks.
I sailed on, while drowned men toppled
Backwards through my frayed ropes and slept.

And now, a lost ship tangled in the hair of coves, I who am
Flung by hurricanes into the birdless ether,
I whose salvage—so much drunken, waterlogged debris—
Would not detain an ironclad or an escort;

Billowing smoke, and free, and garlanded in violet fog,
I who stove in the sky, which smouldered like a wall
Pocked with solar lichen and azure snot—
Sweetmeats prized by poets—

Who hurtled like a bedlam timber, flecked
With small electric moons, and flanked
By black sea-horses under skies of lapis lazuli
Hammered by the solstice into raging cyclones;

I who trembled as I heard the creak of rutting
Behemoths and stacked thunderheads at fifty leagues,

Eternal weaver of the blue quiescence,
I now ache for Europe and its ancient parapets.

I've seen archipelagos of stars; islands whose feverish
Skies are spread above the mariner—are these the boundless
Nights in which you sleep out exile in your millions,
Golden birds, you prophets of our restitution?

I've cried too much, though. Dawns destroy me.
All moons are atrocious, all suns are a grievance:
An acrid passion has warped my sluggish keel.
Let it split! Let me sink without trace!

Do I long for European waters? Only a sullen pond
Where a small, demoralized boy, crouching
In the musk of a provincial evening
Launches his unsteady boat: a butterfly in May.

The languor of the waves has finally reclaimed me.
I can no longer ride in the wake of cotton freighters,
Or tack along the braggart lines of flags and pennants,
Or slink beneath the frightful eyes of prison ships.

You read the title, nervously, out of deference to the author's
sonnet, 'Voyelles', pick the vowels out of it, 'Le-Ba-teau-iv-re', all five,
counting the 'o' sound of 'eau', and then the first line: 'Comme je
descendais des Fleuves impassibles'. Not the English 'impassable' but
'impassibles': impassive, expressionless, inscrutable.—It is the boat,
in its cups, speaking: 'as I was going down', 'I headed down', 'I was
making my way'. This is a naumorphic thing: 'Je' is indeed 'un autre'.
It also marks the beginning of a certain bare-faced insolent tone in
literature—'insolent' from Latin 'solere', to be accustomed to. 'Insolite'
is French for strange or unusual. Here, the sun 'casts its monu-
mental, violet welts of light', oh, like actors in some terribly old
plays, 'de drames très-antiques'. Our poet lives there. His is the terrain

between insolent and unfamiliar. 'I was minding my own business when', 'As I was going down Sackville Street', 'I lived in an L-shaped room',[6] 'I was fairly and squarely behind the eight/ That morning in Foster's pool hall'.[7] The thing is plain-spoken, resolute, correct, and utterly orthodox. It is made of obedience, subsidiary clauses, and a powerful vocabulary. If there's anything unorthodox in it, it's the fact that some simple words are seen to be either unavoidable or favourites, and are repeated, even as the poem as a whole bears the aspect of a museum with glazed dioramas of twenty-five lurid scenes: *vert, bleu, noir, flot, coton, amer, amour, oeil, fleur, enfant, Europe, regretter, noyé*; and that it makes sense, at the place where sense ends.

Because 'Le Bateau Ivre' seems to me such a remote and unaccountable and immense thing, I want to take a step or two back from it at this point. To understand or begin to investigate a poem, I have to understand how it might have come to be written, and of that, with a 16-year-old genius in the French sticks, in 1871, I have no conception. There is a little anticipation of it, then, in the charming 'Les Poètes de Sept Ans', where Rimbaud writes, in the Penguin translation of Jeremy Harding:

> At seven, he was writing romances about life
> In the great desert, where kidnapped Freedom shone,
> Forests, suns, river banks, savannas. He borrowed
> From the illustrated magazines—Spanish and Italian
> Girls smiled out at him; he blushed.[8]

And that is, if you like, one of the identity-foils of the 'Bateau Ivre': it's the work of a precocious dreamer, a star pupil, who even when

naughty is unable to escape his aura of virtue; even while truant-
ing is unable altogether to slip the memory of the *Primusbank*, the
seat reserved for the top boy of the class. 'Le Bateau Ivre' is an odd
marriage between the qualities of Rimbaud's mother Vitalie Cuif,
and his father's: *tüchtig*, hard-working, churchy (Mme Rimbaud
has her own biography, by Francoise Lalande)—and Captain
Rimbaud, who came and went and finally, having sired four
children, stayed away, an officer in the French colonial army.[9] I'm
sure that's one reason why Robert Lowell, with Charlotte Winslow
his own dragon mother and the ill-named Commander Lowell, his
own experience of the absent military father, was drawn to trans-
late Rimbaud. Lowell's version of 'The Poet at Seven' comes imme-
diately before 'The Drunken Boat' in *Imitations*, his book of free
translations of a European anthology from Homer to Pasternak.
Where Rimbaud rolls his eyes at the absurdity of such a thing
and de-personalizes his title—'Les Poètes de Sept Ans': there are
none—Lowell positively lays claim to it—'The Poet at Seven': it's
me. The one is derisive, the other literal. 'The Poet at Seven'
becomes a sort of annex to Lowell's own autobiographical
self-portraits in earlier poems like 'Grandparents' or 'Last
Afternoon with Uncle Devereux Winslow'. With Lowell's upper-
case 'Mother' (which he also used of his own), his self-disgust
curdling almost—but never quite—into comedy, the irregular,
sporadically rhymed lines of *Life Studies*, the negatives and the semi-
colons, his version is less a translation than a makeover of Rimbaud:

> When the timeless, daily, tedious affair
> was over, his Mother shut
> her Bible; her nose was in the air;
> from her summit
> of righteousness, she could not see the boy;

his lumpy forehead knotted
with turmoil, his soul returned to its vomit.[10]

Four even alexandrines makes about three and a half of Lowell's jagged couplets; the approval of simple homework has been turned into an obscure domestic worship ritual; the power and terror of Rimbaud's mother has been turned into the faintly ridiculous (and essentially harmless) priggishness of Lowell's, no longer alive; while the figure of the boy is plainly squalid, some way from Rimbaud's lifelong project of inscrutable hypocrisy, where the eyes—Lowell leaves them out, and later gives them to the Mother, saying 'she had the true blue look that lied', when really it is the boy—where the eyes are not windows but window-dressing for the soul, which is carefully hidden from the all-powerful Mother's prying. This is what gives us the famous Carjat photographs of the teenage Rimbaud, equally expressionless and iconic, suffering and pugnacious, boyish and effeminate. Whereas the Lowell character, however disagreeable, is harmonious, of a piece in its rough charmlessness, we may read of Rimbaud:

and of that charm there's little doubt. Delahaye speaks of him rub-
bing his eyes with his knuckles, like a sleepy child, and blushing if
he were introduced to anyone new. A luminous innocence glim-
mered through the crust of monstrousness he had cultivated so
assiduously.[11]

The Rimbaldian self, as Jeremy Harding writes, is 'a harsh experi-
ment in disfiguring .... It's the imperfect fit that works so well.' In Lowell, the boy's forehead is purely 'lumpy'; in Rimbaud it is *plein d'éminences*, full of elevations, almost—punningly—high-minded.[12] A lot of the joy of 'Les Poètes de Sept Ans' and of 'Le Bateau Ivre' is in their unique and astounding psychological configurations.

They have the clarity, the angles, and the helplessness of a really macabre, eccentric autobiographical novel. The Lowells one knows: slugs and snails and puppy dogs' tails; accumulating turtles in an urn[13] till they stank.

'The Poet at Seven' ends:

> What he liked best were dark things:
> the acrid, dark rings
> on the ceiling, and the high,
> bluish plaster, bald as the sky
> in his bare bedroom, where he could close
> the shutters and lose
> his world for hundreds of hours,
> mooning doggedly
> over his novel, endlessly
> expanding with jaundiced skies,
> drowned vegetations, and carnations
> that flashed like raw flesh
> in the underwater green
> of the jungle starred with flowers—
> dizziness, mania, revulsions, pity!
> Often the town playground
> below him grew loud with children;
> the wind brought him their voices,
> and he lay alone on pieces of unbleached canvas,
> violently breaking into sail.[14]

Some of these words are just pure Lowell: 'mooning', 'mania', 'pity'. They come with invisible copyright signs after them. 'Children' is as exotic and weird coming from Lowell as his occasional 'girls'.[15] (Lowell was an only child; he makes Rimbaud, who had, of all things, an older brother, plus two sisters, seem like one too: an only child.) Offering 'jaundiced', a medical or psychological word, in a meteorological context, is clever; it gives the tropical world some quality of interiority. The play of 'carnations'— etymologically, flesh-flowers—with 'flash' and 'flesh' likewise, 'carnations that flashed like raw flesh'. *'seul, et couché sur des pièces de toile/ écrue et pressentant violemment la voile!'* With violent imaginings of sails as he lay in the sheets. 'He lay in his coarse canvas sheets,/ Gripped by a premonition of setting sail', is how the Penguin 'Seven-Year-Old Poets' ends, where 'canvas', 'sheets', and 'sail' are beautifully synonyms. All these things are aptly destabilizing, confounding. It is a boy intoxicated with his encyclopaedia.

'Le Bateau Ivre' is like the novel the young Rimbaud might have been doggedly mooning over for hundreds of hours (he cleverly doesn't stipulate whether he's reading it or writing it, and indeed, the texture of the finished poem is somewhere between reading and writing), with the drowned vegetation and the underwater green of the jungle and the violent breaking into sail. A sort of Nabokovian poem-within-a-poem, or better, a poem-outside-a-poem. 'Le Bateau Ivre' begins at the end. Human agency, the guides, the *'haleurs'* or haulers, the touch on the tiller, they are all gone. There are no witnesses or survivors. It would ordinarily be the subject for an inquiry, explanations, de-mystification. Instead, the boat is free, has self-determination, can vote and fight and smoke and drink and marry and leave home. (And the greatest of these is leave home.) I'll follow Jeremy Harding's translation:

> On my way down inscrutable Rivers
> My haulers seemed to slacken off the ropes—
> Yelping redskins had takEN GOOD AIM,
> Stripped them and nailed them to painted poles.

The crews and cargo meant nothing to me—
Flemish wheat or English cottons.
The clamour was done with, and so were the haulers.
The Rivers took me downstream as I pleased.

It's like the opening of another Werner Herzog film, *Aguirre, Wrath of God*, only the resemblance I suppose should be seen as going the other way. Perhaps a bit of encyclopaedia-loyalty has preserved the upper case 'R' of '*Rivers*' (and then later the 'P' of '*Peaux-rouges*', and '*Peninsules*' and '*Poème*', the 'M' of '*Maelstroms*', the 'V' of '*Vigueur*', the 'A' of '*Aubes*': they all look as though they've just been looked up. Or written into an illuminated manuscript.). The boat's senses are both sharp and blunt; things that narrowly concern itself, it seems to notice less. Perhaps it is better at taking in things in the distance, anyway. The rivers are '*impassible*'—neutral, indifferent, apathetic. One imagines them as being perhaps shapeless, less rivers than flooded land, as in Elizabeth Bishop's late poem 'Santarem', recalling an Amazon cruise: 'more than anything else I wanted to stay awhile/ in that conflux of two great rivers, Tapajos, Amazon,/ grandly, silently flowing, flowing east.'[16] Then, there are the haulers, *seeming* to slacken; the boat, in a moment of absent-mindedness, has missed what actually happened. Against that, the witnessing of their death- or torture-scene is vivid in the extreme. Vivid and relished. Similarly, it is indifferent to crew and cargo; on the other hand, it registers the quality of the new silence right away, and with some measure of satisfied spite or exasperation. 'Their conversation ended with their lives', is Lowell's hoity-toity version: a droll, rather bloodthirsty, drawing-room account of bloodcurdling screams; in the original, it's the rather plaintive neighbour's '*ont fini ces tapages*'. The row, the din, the kerfuffle. 'For a good voice, hearing is a torture',[17] says Lowell. This is a hypersensitive, neurasthenic boat, a boat with *ennui*, an Axel or Symbolist Des Esseintes among boats. A boat for the Eighties and Nineties. Maybe I could take a moment here to look at the composition of the poem's vocabulary. There are the proper nouns and names, its literal and figurative stars, the 'Marys-of-the-Sea', Floridas, Leviathan, Monitors, Hanseatic, Sirius, Behemoths. There are ship words, such things as ropes, crews, cargo, beacons, hull, rudder, grapnel, my sluggish keel, the 'flanks' or *'bords'*, the *'voiliers'*, the *'planches folles'*; there are words of sea and navigation, the haulers, the rivers, the tempests, tide-rips, water-spouts, waves, breakers, harbour beacons, undertows, reefs and swells, oceans, hurricanes, *gouffres*. There are words from cosmology and geography, if they can be separated, I think they can, the rivers, the drifting peninsulas, small electric moons, stacked thunderheads, archipelagos of stars, coves, a floating island. There is a perhaps surprising abundance of terrestrial words, apples, walls, cattle, panthers, doves, birds, flowers, and so forth. There are words of sky and time, ten nights, dusk and dawn, the low sun, the green night, ether, months, dawns, Julies, moons, evening, May. There are colours, enough colours for several rainbows, redskins, green, bluish, milk-white suspension, *'les azurs verts'*, violet, blue and yellow, rainbow, of course, glaucous, silver, brown, blackness, golden, yellow, black, violet again, azure again, ultramarine, black again, blue again, golden again. There are words of sound, often deafening, tumultuous sound, yelping, clamour, *clapotements, tohu-bohu, rutilements, cataractant*, with a subset of sounds of pain, *sanglots, geindre, pleurer* (sobbing, groaning, weeping). There are words of other senses, of taste and feel and smell, lighter than a cork, sour apples, bluish wine, bitter, drastically fermented rednesses of love, the circulation of bizarre sap, the *sèves inouïes, les noirs parfums, un acre amour.* There are words of motion, toppled and flung, hurtled, hammered, *heurté, traverser, nager,* rolling, climbing, plummet, ran, danced, surged, ride, slink. There are words of intensity, of pitch or scale, words that lay claim, *inouies, lumineux, hysterique, ineffables, incroyable, énormes, atroce, enivrantes.* There are words expressive of an emotional or psychological state or condition: *impassible, pensifs, éveil, délire, mystiques, rêve, hysteriques, martyr lassé, tremblais, regrette, exil, torpeur, langueurs.* Often these are words of exhaustion or enervation.

Even by themselves the array and the diversity are astounding. It feels like an amazingly well-stocked poem, with nary a quiet or neutral or unforceful word in it. (If you like, the opposite of a Robert Frost poem.) It is somehow beyond showing off. The kind of poem that is almost its own concordance—which I think is true. It is a hard poem to hold or to order in the mind; hard to follow minutely the pitch and drama of the thing. Hard to draw or chart its progress across its overwhelmingly self-contained quatrains. For all its constructions—and I said it was made of subclauses—it is as though the poem is poured thickly out of a blender. All its words apply to the boat; I mean, it is all boat, and simultaneously all world; there is no surface, no separation, no skin. What it sees, what it traverses, what it loses, what drops off it, all eventually become its story. The world enters the boat; splinter by splinter, the boat enters the bloodstream of the world. That boast: 'Et j'ai vu quelquefois ce que l'homme a cru voir!' The visionary becomes the haunted. The conclusion suggests itself, inevitably a simplification, that various animates and various inanimates have been thrown together. I can't get that endlessly suggestive sentence of Jeremy Harding's out of my head: 'it's the imperfect fit that works so well.' External and internal, cosmic and topical, accurate and excessive, traumatic and euphoric, hypersensitive and inert. The drunken and the boat. As I say, often it is the things outside that are registered with the most inwardness; the interior—the cargo, the crew—is a matter of blank indifference or hatred. At the same time, though, this is a psychologizing and introspective speaker. He is telling us how he feels, and how an experience feels. It becomes an old boat in a young world. If you can be a vagrant at sea—why not a tramp-steamer—then that. A thing 'all badged with sores', as Heaney says,[18] in a planet that seems chemically and electro-magnetically still in the process of putting itself together. One reads the poem looking for the speaker's absolute centre, the bit that can't be jettisoned, the irreducible thing in it that says 'I'. Because its identity, as well as its experience, seems to lie in depletion, in martyrdom. Is it the quasi-coffin, the 'coque de sapin', the pine-plank hull in line 18? Is it the 'presque ile', the floating island, or the 'bateau perdu' or the 'carcasse ivre d'eau' or the 'planche folle' as it loses being? Is it the two prayers called out near the end, in the antepenultimate stanza: 'O que ma quille éclate! O que j'aille a la mer!' typical of its alert music, the 'y' sound, the play on 'jaillir' to spurt,[19] the droll idea of 'going to sea'—almost of going to seed—while at sea. It reminds one of the idea of le Corbusier that no building is finished until it is standing in ruins. There are perhaps no sober boats.

Because, left to myself, I find the progress of the bateau ivre so confounding, I will gratefully adopt Gerald Macklin's suggestion of a four-part order. According to Macklin, the first five quatrains, lines 1 to 20, are 'setting sail'. The river, the loss of cargo and crew, the first foundational ten-day storm, a rite of passage, the first puncturings and losses. The less function the better; the less weight; the less control. Freedom begins with negatives, negatives and passives: I no longer felt myself guided, meant nothing to me, descend and allowed to descend as I pleased. Then in line 11, the boat starts to 'run'; by line 14 it is dancing; in line 20, it is broken open and washed clean of its *soilure* (its history), and loses '*gouvernail et grappin*', its anchor and rudder, in other words its brakes and steering wheel, its ability to stop and turn, or rather, be stopped and be turned. In keeping with the emancipation of the speaker, there is the amazing broken alexandrine in line 12, where the expected caesura after the sixth syllable would fall slap bang in the middle of the word '*tohu-bohus*'—something like pandemonium— an absolute no-no and scandal in conservative French versification. Airily Robert Lowell wrote to Elizabeth Bishop of Rimbaud, with no evidence: 'I think he rather hated meter and syntax, though a great master of both, while Baudelaire gloried in both.'[20] I think he was probably perfectly wrong. Throughout, the boat speaks like an animal, or a subject species or creature: human beings have enslaved it, there is eternal enmity between it and them. It begins to speak only when its last humans—its keepers, as it were—have been brutally put to death. The transference of physical pain in the poem I think would have interested Kafka. Pain is a currency, to feel or inflict. I hurt, therefore I am. Transitive or intransitive, to taste. While the '*oeil niais des falots*', 'the imbecile blink of harbour beacons' in Harding, 'the crass eye of the lanterns' in Beckett, is a memory, maybe, of the gaoler's peephole.[21]

Lines 21 to 56, stanzas 6 to 14, are assigned by Macklin to the heart of the poem, the voyage proper, the intoxication. '*Et dès lors*', it goes, from then on, thenceforward, and a litany of absorption, intensity, delirium. Here come the colours, the polysyllables, the vocabulary of shock and physical geography, the boastful mixing and mangling of senses, the exclamation marks and the wild disorientation and contradiction. In stanzas 9 to 13, Rimbaud falls into a chanting perfect tense listing of all that the boat has seen and done: *j'ai vu, j'ai rêvé, j'ai suivi, j'ai heurté*, and again *j'ai vu*. The lines and stanzas are mostly centrifugal, sending the reader reeling away into hallucinatory details, the singing phosphorus, the creatures with panthers' eyes and human skin, the underwater rainbows, like some sort of twenty-second-century Herodotus. These are often very beautiful, contrary, mocking, difficult, and beautiful again. The sea as shutters, the sea as cattle, dawn as doves, the waterfall at the edge of the world. Rimbaud seems intent on displaying such virtuosity that he can make anything appear before our eyes, with a taunting You like this? what about this then? and this? We remember his ability to write prize-winning poems in Latin when he was still younger. And it's truly all middle, not false start after false start. The hand, as Brodsky says, combines its existence with that of a head, and fetches more lines.[22] The ghostly slow motion of the drowned man in line 24, '*un noyé pensif parfois descend*', with its mix of callousness and cute observation. Lines of formidable musicality, poise and originality. The occasional bundling like line 32, '*et j'ai vu quelquefois ce que l'homme a cru voir*'—and more than once, is the implication, I've seen things that people delude themselves they've seen.[23] At the end of this entire phantasmagorical sequence, the fourteenth stanza goes spinning away into two verbless sentences of one line and three lines, the one shiny and (never mind the furnace!) essentially cold and needle-sharp, all crystalline Arctic shards: 'glaciers, silver suns, reaches like mother-of-pearl.' The other dull, dark, murky, brackish, contorted, tropical, opaque, evoking the mangroves and

invasive boa constrictors of the Florida—the *'incroyable Florides'*—I
come to you from:

> Hideous wrecks at the bottom of deep, brown sumps
> Where gigantic snakes, maddened by vermin and stinking
> Of blackness, plummet from twisted trees.

And all the maximal nouns, verbs, adjectives, and adverbs of the
categories I started to fill in above.

Lines 57 to 88, stanzas 15 to 22, mark the third phase, labelled
'deceleration and disenchantment' by Macklin, the point, he
says, 'where "Le Bateau Ivre" begins to lose both momentum and
self-belief'. These things are relative, I suppose, and I don't think
it's meant as a criticism, but of course he is right. It is an element
of the performance, the long fourth act, the service break in the
vital seventh game. The poem drifts into the conditional—strangely
so, because it seems so universal and omni-competent and all-
encompassing; it doesn't need the conditional; what could a
conditional possibly have to add to it? Wittgenstein says: 'The pic-
ture represents a possible state of affairs in logical space.'[24] But
now the boat wishes it could show fish to children, then it sees
itself as a woman. We have more drowned sailors, more birds,
more skies. The boat becomes self-conscious, even maudlin,
indulges in pathos-laden and rhetorical evocations of itself:
'moi, bateau perdu', *'moi qui trouais'*, *'planche folle'*, *'moi qui tremblais'*.
It seems, as the conditional suggests, to see itself from a dis-
tance. The surprising mention of Europe in stanza 21 seems to
bear this out. Rimbaud has built a platform in space from which
to look back at himself. There's a sense of dissociation, the first
person flickering back and forth into a spectral third. For the
first time perhaps we think we're in the company of some

centaur-like creature, half-boy, half-boat. A further conditional in stanza 18 claims no ship would bother to pick up 'so much drunken, waterlogged debris'. The proud, active perfects of the second phase of the poem are replaced by languorous, habitual, inescapable imperfects: *'je restais'*, *'je voguais'*, *'qui trouais'*, *'qui courais'*, *'qui tremblais'*. (How different that *'qui courais'*—Harding gives 'hurtled', I think perhaps something like 'flogged'—is from the *'Je courus!'* of line 13! Beckett has 'scudded', at any rate, it's not fun anymore.) At the same time as the boat starts to sound battered, it starts to reflect its boy-author: now considerate of children, now 'like a woman'; now, punningly, anthropomorphically, *'Libre, fumant'*, evoking Verlaine's sketch of Rimbaud (made in June 1872, a year later!) walking with shoulder-length hair under a flat wide-brimmed hat, smoking his pipe; now *'ivre d'eau'*, drunk on water. It is like a magnificent enactment of the gyrations of puberty, yawing from self-adoration to misery; extreme sensitivity to solipsism; grandiosity to smallness. And then when we have the next perfect, in stanza 22, and the return of excitability and magnificence, *'J'ai vu des archipels sidéraux!'* the imperfects seem to have come to an end, and you think you've spent some time in a blind alley, or enclosed in a digression.

Something like that must have occurred to Lowell in his translation in *Imitations*. He must have encountered local difficulties or had trouble—understandably!—working out a coherent and necessary dramaturgy. When he sent Bishop his translations (he dedicated the book of them to her), she wrote back: 'I am very much worried by the French translations, particularly the Rimbaud ones.'[25] Her language is French, Brazilian Portuguese and French. 'I think Baudelaire is more sympathetic to you, verbally, (and probably emotionally) than Rimbaud'—and then rather sweetly, because of course there practically is only early Rimbaud—'at least those early Rimbauds you've chosen'.[26] His translation of the hundred-line poem is just sixty lines long. His version takes just fifteen out of the original's twenty-five stanzas. He reverses the order of the 4th and 5th; keeps just four of the nine of Macklin's second section, going 13, 18, 15/16, 22; cuts the eight of the third to a mere three; and keeps only the brief last part intact, and even that, to me, seems to have problems.

The fourth part, lines 89 to 100, stanzas 23 to 25, is assigned, as per Macklin, to 'closure'. The feeling of *taedium vitae* and abjectness becomes overwhelming: '*toute lune est atroce et tout soleil amer.*' Each of the three stanzas makes somehow its own end. Each is differently conclusive. Perhaps Rimbaud is still playing his You like this? game with the reader—what about this? It's difficult, almost painful, to break from one to the other—it's like encountering a sequence of three close-brackets. Three bolts are slid. Three lids nailed down. Three deadlocks turned. First the wish, the volatile, theatrical, flyaway ejaculation: 'Let me sink without trace!' 'O that my keel might break, and I might drown!' says Lowell, echoing his Leopardi translation (also in *Imitations*) of 'The Infinite': 'It's sweet to destroy my mind/ and go down/ and wreck in this sea where I drown.'[27] Next, there is the 'small', reverse ending, somewhere probably close to the actual circumstances of the writer, the frustrated dreamer hunkered with a toy boat beside a pond, the least possible sea, the 'small, demoralized boy, crouching/ in the musk of a provincial evening'. Small, small, inconsequential, no names, no colours, no magnificence. It is like the small death of the eel, back from its heroic life in the Sargasso.[28] The Rimbaud and Mallarmé scholar Robert Greer Cohn sees 'this little quatrain' as 'perhaps without peer in any literature',[29] and says: 'The most tactful comment here is silence.'[30] Interestingly, an early German translation, by Paul Zech, twenty-eight stanzas long, took it upon itself to reverse the order of the final two stanzas. As I suggest, I see why. It is the most delicate and suggestive ending. Then there is stanza 25, which takes us back to the negatives of the beginning, the protestations of incapacity or inability, 'I can no longer... or... or...'. Alan Jenkins's brilliantly rhymed and syntactically broken version goes:[31]

> Steeped in the languorous swell, I can't any more
> Tack in the big barges' wake, lift the clipper's prize
> Or breast the proud flags and the flapping pennants; nor
> Drift past the prison hulks, beneath their hollow eyes.

We are back in the prison of the 'oeil niais', back with the 'haleurs', and the 'grappin' and 'gouvernail'. Left with the international situation of 1871, in the world of trade, of Red Ensigns, of prison ships, the defeat of the French in the Franco-Prussian War, the brutal government crackdown, as we now say, after the Paris Commune. Left with the adolescent's posture of refusal: shan't, shan't, shan't.

Rimbaud's qualities in 'Le Bateau Ivre', the correctness and copiousness and seeming orderliness of the poem, the loosely or chancily connected stanzas, the high colours and strong impressions, the detailed phases of an irresistible process, the taking down of one's own cell-walls the better to speak of the universe, all these make a reappearance, rather soon, and in German, in some of the early poems of Bertolt Brecht. The first-person, 'The Ship', written in 1919, when Brecht was 21, is very identifiably a translation, even though Rimbaud's quatrains have become sestets and the leaky, creaking ship doubles as Brecht's then heavily pregnant girl-friend, Paula Banholzer. I quote # 4 and # 5 of the six:

> Into my timbers in the fourth moon
> Seaweed drifted, the joists blossomed green:
> Again my face became another while
> Green and wafting in the guts slowly
> I voyaged on, not suffering much, heavy
> With moon and vegetation, shark and whale.
>
> To gulls and weed I was a place of rest
> Not rescue, guiltless nevertheless.
> Heavy and full I'll be when I go down.
> Now in the eighth month oftener
> Waters trickle into me. My face is paler
> And I ask that it will finish soon.[32]

The zestful morbidity to be found in the early Brecht—with pale, green, washed-out, and rotten among his favourite attributes— surely owes everything to Rimbaud. 'Ballad on Many Ships', 'Ballad of Cortez' Men', 'Ballad of the Pirates', and many others follow in the same manner. You could almost describe them as a conflation of Rimbaud the poet, and the later African adventurer. In 1919, Brecht, who also read and imbibed Kipling—tippling Kipling, to the extent that he was dubbed 'Rudyard' Brecht on occasion—displays a greater knowingness with reference to late-colonial wars and understands that empires are founded on the bones of dead soldiers. He almost deliberately set life aside and dwelt on a kind of phosphorescent death-in-life, in 'The Liebestod Ballad' and in 'The drowned girl'. It is organic and physical, the dramatization of a rare state of continued or attenuated being, an entropic Ophelia:

1

When she had drowned and begun her drifting down
Out of the streams into the greater rivers
The opal of the sky shone with a wondrous sheen
As though it must appease this corpse of hers.

2

Weed and algae clung fast to her so she
Little by little became much heavier
The swimming fish touched her legs coolly
Plants and beasts on her last voyage further weighted her.

3

And the sky in the evening became as dark as smoke
And at night with the stars it kept the light pending.
But early enough and brightly day broke
So that there should still be for her a morning and an evening.

4

When her pale body had rotted in the water
God's slow and gradual forgetting of her began:
First her face, then her hands and last of all her hair.
Then she became carrion in rivers with much carrion.[33]

Perhaps this drowned thing is the ideal poem, with pathos and beauty and a little horror, for the novelty; variously biodegradable, the tartar on the teeth already fossil; hospitable, adaptive, welcoming, undefendable, bogging down, losing its essence to the water, and acquiring other, foreign contents; unconcerned with safe arrival or with commerce; facing no suits for authorship or against plagiarism, forgotten even by God. And that's literature, 'carrion in rivers with much carrion'.

3

EUGENIO MONTALE

'Barche sulla Marna', *'Boats on the Marne'*

For a long time, I've thought the three principal books of the Italian Nobel laureate Eugenio Montale (1896–1981) had a sort of ideal chronological arrangement. There was *Ossi di Seppia* (Cuttlefish Bones) of 1925, when he was still in his 20s; *Le Occasioni* (The Occasions) of 1939, fourteen years later; and *La Bufera e altro* (The Storm and Others) in 1956, when he turned 60. The books have the space, the distanciation, the sheer occupation of the crease otherwise accorded to reigns or wars; these things are not going to be superseded; where is the 'breaking news' ribbon that is going to eclipse or invalidate them? These three books—often published together as one *Collected Poems 1920–1954*, as by his American translator Jonathan Galassi, or by Hanno Helbling in German—are the books of his life, and, at four or five hundred pages in their parallel text editions, none too shabby; these are the books and the production and arrangement and occupation I mean. As the poet wrote later: 'I consider my three books as three canticles, three phases of a human life.'[1] One doesn't want to over-burden the reader's capacity or memory. After the third of them, one reads that Montale took 'a long break from writing poetry'; as when not, you may imagine. He was then lucky enough to publish four final collections in his last ten years: *Satura, Diario del '71 e del '72, Quaderno di quattro anni,* and *Altri versi e poesie disperse*. These are sometimes called the *'retrobottega'* or 'back of the store' collections; I'd even offer the incorrect 'back of the envelope' as a possible translation for *'retrobottega'*. 'I've written one single book, of which I gave the *recto* first, now I'm giving the *verso*',[2] he said. A new informality, scruffiness, demystification, drollness. Sometime during this efflorescence, in 1975, he was awarded his Nobel Prize. He died in Milan, at the age of 85, in 1981.

Back up, then. In this slow Forties cinematic zoom, from globe to map to topographical Ordnance Survey, the book I am interested in is Montale's second, *Le Occasioni,* 'The Occasions'. The modesty of it (poetry depending on its 'occasions'); the swagger or claim of it (these are the moments that matter); the straightforwardness of it (these poems had to be written). Like the books of Montale's preceding and following it (the two following it, in fact), *Le Occasioni* comes with an internal organization. This has an odd effect. The poems are not lost or stuffed in a sack, they are located in a sort of crystalline way. Almost like the child's address: flat, house, street, postal district, town, county, country, continent, hemisphere. One might think of Baudelaire's *Fleurs du Mal*—the different women, the different themes of Spleen and Ideal—or Lowell's *Life Studies,* bringing himself up to date through its four sections. A poem in a sequence comes with a sense of purpose or design that one in an uncharted, unpartitioned book may not have. It's always a question with poems: can they play with others or are they monopolistic, saying in effect, 'thou shalt have no other poems save only me'.

Le Occasioni has four parts. Or even a proem and four parts. Because 'The Balcony' was lifted out of the Motets and set at the head of the book. There follows a first section of sixteen poems; then the Motets, short poems, twenty of them; then the single poem 'Tempi di Bellosguardo', three pages long, in three parts; and then section four of fifteen poems, of which our poem, 'Barche Sulla Marna' comes in tenth spot. Pessimism or letting-go can of course come at any moment in a poet like Montale; already in the book (which begins with someone, maybe the poet, at an unlit window), we've had: 'dances no more', 'the last herd', 'But it's late, always later', 'And Hell is certain', 'and time passes', 'Life which seemed/ immense, is smaller than your handkerchief'.³ I recall a woman waving goodbye, in Andrew Motion's *Independence*, in 'a sinking cloud of dust'. Still, whether each section is its own bell-curve, or the four of them together make up one such, a poem coming two-thirds of the way through the fourth and last part of a book is going to have something—as we say in German, a little word—to say about lateness. '*il vento che tarde, la morte, la morte que vive!*' to quote 'Notizie dall'Amiata', 'the wind that lingers, death, the death that lives!'⁴

Le Occasioni, and a lot of the paradoxes and oxymorons in it and the Dante in it, may be laid at the feet of Irma Brandeis—*nomen est omen*, Brand/eis, ice/fire, 'sap check'd with frost, and lusty leaves quite gone/ Beauty o'ersnow'd and bareness every where'⁵ as the Shakespearean epigraph goes to Part IV, our part—Irma Brandeis, a young Jewish American Dante scholar who turned up at Montale's place of work, the Vieusseux library in Florence. This was in April 1933. 'August, travels to London, Eastbourne and Paris.' The next date I have is 1938, which goes, in full: 'Marianna, his beloved sister, dies. May, Hitler in Florence. July, racial laws are enacted in Italy. December, forced to resign his post at the Vieusseux for failing to join the Fascist Party. Makes plans to join

Brandeis in the States, to which she has returned, but does not leave Italy.' 1939 is, in part, 'Publication of *Le Occasioni*, his second book'. Biographical information on Montale seems to be at a premium in English; this comes from a four-page 'Table of Dates' in Harry Thomas's 2002 Penguin sampling of Montale translations, which is about all I have to go on.[6]

Montale is proposed to one rather bullyingly as a hermeticist poet, and accordingly there is a vast gulf between what one sees and instinctively responds to and thinks one understands in the pages of his poems, and what is given in notes at the back of books, which can be almost frivolously eclectic, information in its decadent phase. I make a point of resisting this because I don't like to see what I take to be a poetry of heart and body disappear into the sort of confected realm of intellectualism and allusion. It's a little like the experience of reading Chinese poetry in old Penguin paperback editions. A delicate four-line poem sits on a page of small-point/*petit-point* annotation like a basil leaf on a sinological doorstop. Things that looked to one perfectly urgent and 'real' are given a ridiculous gamesome flavour, really, as though they had been done for a dare, or a coterie. Montale himself abets this, with his comments, equally earnest and abstruse, on the poems and how they came to be written. Commenting 'I was rarely at Bellosguardo'.[7] Letting us know that the coastguard house in the poem of that name was destroyed when the poet was 6 years old[8]; that 'Dora Markus' was based on the photograph of a woman's legs that a friend sent him,[9] and so forth. Elsewhere, though, he writes: 'There is a middle road between understanding nothing and understanding too much, a *juste milieu* which poets instinctively respect more than their critics; but on this side or that of the border there is no safety for either poetry or criticism. There is only a wasteland, too dark or too bright.'[10] Here and always, I hope to be on this middle road, in which I deeply believe.

Le Occasioni is, or became, the book of Irma Brandeis. I had thought, accordingly, for a very long time, that she was everywhere in it, and, in those years, with him; that in their affair or association, complications, hindrances, reservations, were few and technical; somehow almost aleatory or even voluntary. That Irma Brandeis, or 'Clizia' to give her her heroic Montalean alias, was everywhere, the frozen flame behind every 'tu'. Then, that in 1938 we suddenly had the Casablanca ending—God knows, there were alternatives—and Montale remained behind on the Italian tarmac. 'but does not leave Italy.' This was the sense I took to 'Barche sulla Marna', dated '1933/1937' in Arrowsmith's notes, and elsewhere. I supposed they would have gone there together, under the general rubric of 'Paris' in 1933, just as the poem 'Eastbourne' would have come about when they visited Eastbourne that same year; I went so far as to look up Irma's birthday—no, 3 February— and her saint's day, on 9 July, which is just about a possibility for the 'di della tua festa'. Arrowsmith talks of 'the great "public-private" poems of the third and fourth sections' of Le Occasioni.[11] After years of believing it is somewhere on the 'private' end of Montale's 'public-private' rainbow, I am changing my mind, and incline to see it as more cosmic-synoptic.

By blind good fortune, because learned Italian sources and Italian commentary are not in my gift or part of my remit, I saw there was a book published in Italian in 2006, a posthumous edition of Montale's Lettere a Clizia, which had the effect of multiplying—even through guesswork and cognates and the occasional playful and passionate English of his letters—my biographical understanding.[12] Thus, as early as the third letter, dated 7 August 1933,[13] he writes to tell Brandeis that he has survived the Bank Holiday (Eastbourne!), if only just, that he feels '*molto molto molto male*', and that if she writes to him poste restante, that would be '*una grande consolazione*'. There follows, in English, the following:

The case with four solutions
(A novel)
1st: Irma   living in Europe
2nd: Arsenio " " U.S.A. (difficult!)
3rd: I. and I. meeting every summer in Europe (horrible winters!!)
4th: A. forgotten and blown to pieces.
Choose, my dearest Irma.

'Arsenio' is an alias for Montale himself, the figure in an earlier poem of his of that name, added to a second edition of *Ossi di Seppia*. The other thing I took from the letters is a late statement, happily in English, of Irma Brandeis's, dated August 1979, the last paragraph of which reads, in full:

In 1931 Leo Ferrero read me some of the poems in the Ossi di Seppia. I cannot say here what they meant to me then. But in 1933 I went to the Vieusseux Library and asked to see E.M. There was a disastrously stupid meeting which should have ended our acquaintance. I do not remember how we overpassed that. We saw each other every day, and wrote to each other every week when I came back to the U.S. in September, to my teaching job. In 1934 I returned to Florence, and learned *for the first time* of Mosca's existence. From the moment she learned of mine, and that we wanted to marry, she was implacable. She promised to kill herself. Her love for him saw no reason not to torture him—and so she did. She wrote me a vile letter which I hope to attach to these others. She forced him to write me a parting letter—and he did so, warning me of it beforehand and asking me to disregard it, to understand it as necessary to prevent her death. She exacted a promise that he would not see me again, and in 1938 he would have kept that promise had a mutual friend not interceded. When I came home at the end of that summer, I knew we would not see one another again as well as I knew that there would be war.[14]

'Mosca', 'the fly', 'for her littleness and nearsightedness',[15] is Drusilla Tanzi, whom Montale knew from 1929; they lived together from 1939, and they were married just before her death in 1963. He seems to have been with Mosca, or it was with Mosca that he seems to have been, during at least part of the summer of 1933, when he wrote 'Eastbourne' and 'Barche sulla Marna'. Altogether, this new knowledge, or distracting part-knowledge, has the effect of taking 'Clizia' and removing her from 'I.B.' and putting her somewhere closer to Petrarch's Laura (or, as John Berryman says, 'something like her') or Dante's Beatrice. A critic called her a Jewish American Beatrice. A mythic dame.

Barche sulla Marna

Felicità del sùghero abbandonato
alla corrente
che stempra attorno i ponti rovesciati
e il plenilunio pallido nel sole:
barche sul fiume, agili nell'estate
e un murmure stagnante di città.
Segui coi remi il prato se il cacciatore
di farfalle vi giunge con la sua rete,
l'alberaia sul muro dove il sangue
del drago si ripete nel cinabro.

Voci sul fiume, scoppi dalle rive,
o ritmico scandire di piroghe
nel vespero che cola
tra le chiome dei noci, ma dov'è

la lenta processione di stagioni
che fu un'alba infinita e senza strade,
dov'è la lunga attesa e qual è il nome
del vuoto che ci invade?

Il sogno è questo: un vasto,
interminato giorno che rifonde
tra gli argini, quasi immobile, il suo bagliore
e ad ogni svolta il buon lavoro dell'uomo,
il domani velato che non fa orrore.
E altro ancora era il sogno, ma il suo riflesso
fermo sull'acqua in fuga, sotto il nido
del pendolino, aereo e inaccessibile,
era silenzio altissimo nel grido
concorde del meriggio ed un mattino
più lungo era la sera, il gran fermento
era grande riposo.
                Qui...il colore
che resiste è del topo che ha saltato
tra i giunchi o col suo spruzzo di metallo
velenoso, lo storno che sparisce
tra i fumi della riva.
                Un altro giorno,
ripeti—o che ripeti? E dove porta
questa bocca che brùlica in un getto
solo?
          La sera è questa. Ora possiamo
scendere fino a che s'accenda l'Orsa.

(Barche sulla Marna, domenicali, in corsa
nel dì della tua festa.)

William Arrowsmith's translation

          Boats on the Marne

Bliss of cork bark abandoned
to the current
that melts around bridges upside down,

and the full moon pale in sunlight:
boats on the river, nimble, in summer
and a lazy murmur of city.
You row along the field where the butterfly
catcher comes with his net,
the thicket across the wall where the dragon's
blood repeats itself in cinnabar.

Voices from the river, cries from the banks,
or the rhythmic stroking of canoes
in the twilight filtering through
the walnut leaves, but where
is the slow parade of the seasons
which was a dawn that never ended, with no roads,
where is the long expectation, and what is the name
of the void that invades us?

The dream is this: a vast
unending day, almost motionless,
that suffuses its splendor between the banks
and at every bend the good works of man,
the veiled tomorrow that holds no horror.
And the dream was more, more, but its reflection
stilled on the racing water, under
the oriole's nest, airy, out of reach,
was one high silence in the noontime's
rhyming cry, and the evening
was a long morning, the great turmoil
great repose.
                    Here…the color that endures
is the gray of the mouse that leapt
through the rushes or the starling, a spurt
of poison metal disappearing
in mists along the bank.
                    Another day,
you were saying—what were you saying? And where
does it take us, this river mouth gathering in a single
rush?

This is the evening. Now we can descend
downstream where the Great Bear is shining.

(Boats on the Marne, on a Sunday outing
on your birthday, floating.)

As Robert Lowell I think says somewhere—it is a classic trope—
there is nothing so sad as the memory of good times in bad.
Accordingly, 'Boats on the Marne' begins with the word 'Felicità',
happiness, *bonheur*, *Glück*. It sounds a little like a toast or a blessing,
there's only a difference in the preposition: happiness to the cork,
happiness of the cork. But it's not a benediction, it's what gram-
marians call a noun-phrase and Americans a sentence fragment.
Bliss of the cork, and then a heap of adjectival or adverbial qualifi-
cations. A fragment sounds like a stumpy, abbreviated construc-
tion. But this is a luxuriant fragment, an inclusive fragment, a
fragment full of grammatical ups and downs, in which the corky
subject seems just about the least thing, given that the phrase ends
with the sun in line 4, and the sentence with the city in line 6. The
construction is a sort of seesaw of agency, powerful nouns come
in only to become grammatical objects or to be countermanded
by other nouns:

Bliss of cork bark abandoned
to the current
that melts around bridges upside down,
and the full moon pale in sunlight:
boats on the river, nimble, in summer
and a lazy murmur of city.

Montale is maybe playing pooh-sticks, the game of destinies.
Your stick or mine, your cork or mine. The subject is buoyancy,

which is a useful quality to have, though usually in circumstances you wouldn't want to be in. The cork appears only to disappear again, in nothing flat. It prefigures the shape left by the poem, i.e. washed downstream. 'abandoned' is one of those words, like 'sanction' or 'cleave', that contains its opposite. It might have read, more conclusively, 'discarded' or 'rejected' or 'tossed'. 'The most abandoned lover', I remember rendering the phrase in a piece by Hugo von Hofmannsthal, and wincing at the ambivalence I had produced. That's what this poem is about. After all, doesn't it begin with 'Felicità'.

Power shifts through the sentence. 'Felicità' hands it on to 'sugghero', because it is the property of the cork; the cork is abandoned to the current, but then the current 'melts' around 'bridges', which briefly become the dominant, only they in turn are 'upside down'. And then there is the grammatically unsituated 'e il plenilunio', which briefly takes charge, only that too is devalued by being made 'pale in sunlight', and in fact is nothing much more than a cork itself, a spot, circular and adrift. The whole four lines are a dramatization of transience, perhaps of passivity. You look in the original for a dominant sound or syllable, of the kind that many poems have, starting out, and there really isn't one. This is Heraclitus for hardcore Heracliteans. Nothing gets into this stream without being remade or unmade. Not even once.[16] The verbs are verbs of unmaking: abandoned and melts; even 'upside down' ('rovesciati') and 'pale' (made pale, turned pale, of a contrasting, or, in the English phrase, 'interesting' pallor) are quasi-verbs as well. And then you get a colon. Maybe or maybe not the Japanese haiku colon of 'equals', maybe just a break, and then the first statement of the real subject, the boats of the title, the 'barche'. It's both a break, and not a break.

Whatever was established in the first four lines still obtains. The first part, a gathering of impressions, the background being assembled; then the theme. It takes the camera a little while to light on the hero, or to find the central action it will follow. On the river, in the summer, severe limitations of place and time (these boats are '*agili*' but only '*nell'estate*' just as all life's glory is, as the poet says, 'something with a girl in summer') but in the background which maybe is where authority is, or force, or population, or perhaps history, because that's where the irreducible, unreachable thing is, hangs the city with its perverse '*murmure stagnante*'—its stale, torpid, lazy, and natural-sounding, nature-imitating, murmur, quite enough to override or annul the brisk current. We are back at zero. Or maybe below, because the negative forces have countermanded everything, and the '*felicità*' of the opening is buried. Is barely a memory.

At the end of six lines—six lines perversely, weirdly, almost exhaustingly full of action—we get our first verb. '*Segui*', follow; '*segui coi remi*', follow with your oars, row. An imperative to the reader, or perhaps from the poet to himself. This is a poem actually so unpopulated that others, strangers, are invited into it. An 'I-you' poem, but only just, and nowhere a 'we' poem, save in the verb form of '*possiamo/ scendere*' near the end, 'we can descend', where the 'we' is anything from 'me-plus-one' to 'humanity'. He or she or they are directing their craft, the boat of their life. Perhaps it doesn't matter anyway.

> You row along the field where the butterfly
> catcher comes with his net,
> the thicket across the wall where the dragon's
> blood repeats itself in cinnabar.

'*segui*'—not the most valorous or forceful of verbs. A hint, probably, then of downstream, where the cork went so happily, and a strange sense of being enclosed, so that the things of the land, the banks, concern one as much as those of the water did in the first six lines. They are making progress by water, that might—perhaps even should—as well have been made on foot, or on a bicycle. And accordingly seeing the things of the land, the butterfly hunter, the red foliage or the red creeper. The fact of water gives the progress of our unspoken, maybe non-existent couple an element of luxury (choice) and uncertainty. The bobbing cork and the sun and the butterfly hunter, not to mention the Sunday at the end [the beautiful adjectival form, '*domenicali*', in the original, out of reach of English, it would take a word like 'paschal' to have a comparable effect], all seek to define this as a pleasure outing. Galassi believes, here and later, that there are races going on, which would lend an extra touch of weekend; also of popular hysteria, tension, distraction. It might be worth noting that the poem called 'Buffalo', much earlier on in *Le Occasioni*, is named for a six-day cycle race-track in Paris: Montale seems not averse to sports. Arrowsmith seems not to be interested in the possibility. If it were here, in Oxford, we would have punts. Of course, water was always the uncertain element, from ancient times, and earlier. You prayed to god before you went out on it, and thanked him when you safely got off it. Poseidon or whomever. The Persians would only get on a boat when it was lashed together with other boats, when they had made a bridge across the Hellespont, when they had made it into virtual land—the 'pontoon' of Rimbaud. The idea of risk is in play here throughout. Certainly, uncertainty. Perhaps it's there too in the odd bifurcation:

on the one hand, butterfly, on the other, dragon. About as wide a gulf as nature offers. The butterfly hunter, given an extra, mock-heroic effect by the way in Italian the line breaks on '*cacciatore*', a vision of Nabokov with his net or Jacques Tati as Monsieur Hulot with his deadly stabbing racquet. The poem's air of indeterminacy, or unpredictability is strengthened. Its essence, like the ball's on the roulette wheel, is motion: comic or epic; pleasure or risk; butterfly or dragon. Some binary. War or peace. Ice or fire. It's hard to know exactly what we're looking at here, maybe a wash of Virginia creeper across a brick wall, some play of red on red. 'along the stand of trees beside the wall' is Galassi's suggestion; 'the thicket across the wall where the dragon's/ blood repeats itself in cinnabar', Arrowsmith's. We think we have been looking at something scrupulously, photographically accurate, and feel a little irked here; strange how much the phrasing matters. It reminds us of the slippage, the influencings that have been in progress throughout the poem: the bobbing, the reflections, the repetition, the replenishments, the dual light of sun and moon—literally, twilight—the murmur of the city. Everything thus far has been a spreading, a straying, a seep, a wash. The poem has been making itself before our watching eyes, a poem-*fleuve*, a poem-painting, sifting and settling, a dab here and a dab there, *tachiste*, down to the arrestingly, provocatively, painterly word 'cinnabar'. Whatever cinnabar is.

When the poem resumes, it resumes in the same bunched-together noun-phrase-in-parallel mode, 'Voices from the river, cries from the banks/ or the rhythmic stroking of canoes'. The attention is widening, taking in more at once, in less detail, as the motion of the poem goes into a very characteristic Montalean spiral, from the cork, to the current, to the banks, to a stir of everything at once. (*Le Occasioni* is full of spirals and revolvings.) The sound of the oars comes synaesthetically in a kind of wonderfully encumbered stumble, through the filtered light in the leaves: 'the rhythmic stroking of canoes/ in the twilight filtering through/ the walnut leaves.' There is a confusion, something holistic, blending. Ever since I learned that Yeats could hardly see his hand in front of his face, I understood there's a reason there is Celtic Twilight. Poets with poor eyesight make the most of it. If there is such a thing as poetic justice, there is also poetic eyesight. Anyway, this is how the poem will go on till the end now, in a widening motion, a funnel.

Then, a little surprisingly, the statements—constatations, observations, details—give rise to questions. Oddly unrelated questions, and questions upon questions. The form, the structure, is: we have this and this, but what about that? 'where/ is the slow parade of the seasons/ which was a dawn that never ended, with no roads,/ where is the long expectation/ and what is the name/ of the void that invades us?' (Hard not to think: 'invoids us.' A little unhappy here, Arrowsmith.) And what is it, anyway, you might think, with these questions. There is a kind of unease, an unwellness that is suddenly being voiced here. It sounds almost like ingratitude. Because so far, everything seems to have been if not roses, then at least, a sort of *plein air* outing mode, somehow alongside the action, alongside the banks, alongside the rhythmic canoes, lots to look at, lots to see, a sense of plenitude. Tremendous distraction. 'Poor pulsing fete champetre' says, again, Lowell, on similar terrain to this, from the sound of it. But whatever it was, it hasn't supplied whatever the questions are asking for, principally scale, a certainty of prospect, the ability to proceed in a straight line in any direction. Suddenly the idea of the river speaks to the opposite of these: to smallness, an inability to select, almost a feeling of entrapment. And even if these do not arise from the river, then at least the river has been helpless to prevent them from arising. There is something corrosive about time itself (where is the dawn that never ended), or perhaps about human action. As I said the other day, maybe all boats are drunk. Where is their *gouvernail*, where is their *grappin*? This river feels abruptly like a drain. Mutability, futility, doom of one kind or another. As there is not really a personal speaker yet—things have been registered omnisciently and impersonally so far—these passionately voiced objections don't seem to have surged from any individual mind or heart. They arrive from nowhere, and are suddenly, destructively, everywhere: 'what is the name/ of the void that invades us' says the Arrowsmith translation; 'what do we call/ this emptiness invading us', the Galassi. One might note that there is no 'we' as such in the Italian—'*ci*', it says, 'here'. As I said, it is an 'I-you' poem, not a 'we' poem; one and a small fraction, not two. The use of 'we' proposes a false subject, and a false object, to my mind.

Anyway, the poem then seems to oblige. It understands that we have had a volley of questions launched at us, that we are at a loss to answer or even understand; and with an air of patience, saying, seemingly, more than it needs to, to allay our worries, it expansively begins again: 'The dream is this', '*Il sogno è questo*'. It picks up the 'unending'—the '*alba infinita*' transmuted to an '*interminato giorno*'—and then, a little unexpectedly (but then a lot about this poem is unanticipable, and indeed, as Montale sagely, dryly informs us, that's the thing about poetry, it's 'less predictable than prose'),[17] settles us into our actual or acute physical position, 'between the banks' and the good works of man, the winding river and the veiled tomorrow that holds no terror. The picture is of a sort of benign zigzag, a colourful meander. We can read a description by Montale of a suggestively similar configuration in a letter to a friend, about another poem: 'What has the millrace stolen from you? And who knows it? The little of me that (As little of me as) what is happening here can bring you, as little (or even less) of you as the millrace, the rivulet, the trickle that runs in its bed, its cement trough, can bring me (steal from you).'[18] Whoever it was who started this boat-ride— whichever unhappy cork—he came with baggage. Perhaps he was looking forward to the Impressionist Marne—a scene out of Manet or Monet or Seurat or Corot—and found that he had stayed on into the 1915 battle. (Montale fought in World War I, on the so-called southern front, against the Austrians.) 'horror' seems to settle for nothing less. And maybe the whole idea of staying on, and perhaps overstaying seems to have something to say in the poem.

The helpful poem continues helpfully. 'And the dream was more, more.' The tense has changed, but such things happen in the best of poems. Perhaps the entire movement of the poem can be encapsulated in that space, the discrepant space between 'is' and 'was'. Somewhere between the 'is' and the 'was', the dreamer has awoken. A thing is all around us and in front of us in a 'lunga attesa', a 'long expectation'; then it is behind us, do you know, and it didn't amount to much anyway. From in front it's freedom; necessity in hindsight. 'Eastbourne', which looks to me to operate in a very similar way, to enact a very similar movement of maybe disenchantment, ends with 'embers of the bitter brand that was/ Bank Holiday'.—'che gia fu/ Bank Holiday.' G.S. Fraser's translation even italicizes the 'was'. Something that shines in prospect somehow acquires weight and drabness, and is left behind. In a way, the poem enacts its dates: it is 1933, and happens in real time, a real poem about a real outing. And it is 1937, the thing is a memory, many circumstances have changed, and as John Berryman says at the end of Dream Song 7, called '"The Prisoner of Shark Island", with Paul Muni', a poem about childhood and innocence and not understanding what is put to one: 'for the rats/ have moved in, mostly, and this is for real.'

But I am slightly getting ahead of myself. 'the dream was more, more', and then again 'but', '*ma*'. A poem of 'and' seems to have turned into a poem of 'but'. Montale returns us to the physical setting: 'its reflection/ stilled on the racing water', the kind of paradox Montale loves. Both aspects are given a negative reading: 'stilled' and 'racing'; the qualities are clarity and speed; they might easily have been positives. Here, the feeling is of a sooth-sayer looking into a glass, and something menacing emerging, darkening, clouding over, filling with foreboding. The evenly, smoothly moving water shows an almost palpable image, 'its reflection/ stilled on the racing water'. Here, if Montale used semi-colons, or used them in this poem, there might have been one; instead there is what I'd call the continental comma, the comma splice, a hitch to different action, some of what gives this poem its out-of-breath menace and unpredictability. 'Under/ the oriole's nest, airy, out of reach,/ was one high silence in the noontime's/ rhyming cry.' The times really are all over the place; are we morning, noon, or night? All seem possible. (This too is part of the widening of the poem.) And the translation begins to matter, or to matter more. 'rhyming' is '*concorde*', 'cry' is '*grido*'—not '*scoppi*' as above. '*Grido*' is another word from the Montalean lexicon, '*Sere di gridi, quando l'altalena*', the ineffably beautiful opening of '*Bassa marea*', 'Low Tide', 'Evenings of cries, when the swing'. I would guess a '*grido*' is sharper than a '*scoppo*', a scream rather than a call. There is a Lowell poem called 'The Scream', that, he says, 'owes everything Elizabeth Bishop's calm, beautiful story "In the Village".' There is an Antonioni film, 'Il Grido'. I have a poem that has 'over the hedge the pool where the dentist's children screamed'. That kind of thing. Lowell borrows the oriole for his poem, 'Fall 1961' about his move from Boston to New York, and the atomic clock moving to one minute to midnight for the Cuban Missile Crisis.

> Back and forth!
> Back and forth, back and forth—
> my one point of rest
> is the orange and black
> oriole's swinging nest!

The oriole and the anticipation of war. (The strange Dutch word for war is '*oorlog*'.) Montale has the expressive and variegated nature of a countryman or a small boy. His poems are like a disbanded Noah's Ark, you see loads of creatures everywhere. Birds especially. Swallows, geese, partridges, kestrels, snipe, swans, storks, doves, starlings, house-martins, green woodpeckers, nightbirds, and birds of passage; but also horses, carp, gnats, butterflies, a dachshund, squirrels, eels, frogs, two jackals, mullet, a shark, lizards, dragonflies, a bee-swarm, spiders, tarantulas, moths, a mouse (or rat), a nervous dog, long-eared dogs, a lion-coloured dog, pigs, Unicorn and Tortoise, Goose and Giraffe, worms, trout, porcupines, donkeys (all, and more, in *Le Occasioni*). Montale says it with creatures, their tendency, their symbolic or suggestive or atomic value. I think I've twice seen an oriole in my life; they are, as Lowell says, orange and black, and they eat orange slices, it's *idem per idem*:

> And the dream was more, more, but its reflection
> stilled on the racing water, under
> the oriole's nest, airy, out of reach,
> was one high silence in the noontime's
> rhyming cry, and the evening
> was a long morning, the great turmoil
> great repose.

Era…aereo…era…era…sera…era…. The sounds thread their way through lines 24–30 (like Les Murray's 'Bats' Ultrasound', 'a rare ear, our aery Yahweh'),[19] a sort of celestial being, things warped into their kindly opposites, the nest a 'silence in the noontime's/ rhyming cry, and the evening/ was a long morning, the great turmoil/ great repose'. That's as far as the dream goes. Reality kicks in, the poem starts to fray in appearance, the 'qui', 'Here, with the unspoken adversative before it, *'ma qui…'* 'whereas here…':

> Here…the color that endures
> is the gray of the mouse that leapt
> through the rushes or the starling, a spurt
> of poison metal disappearing
> in mists along the bank.

More creatures, and a kind of glum menace, the mouse (or rat), the rushes, the awful and spectacular starling, memorably, unforgettably described, as though by Keats, a cockney starling, 'a spurt of poison metal', nature's utilitarian proletarians, nature's privates, nature's survivors. And man's familiars. What we want, and what we get. The cinnabar and the butterflies; the oriole; the mouse (or rat) and the starlings. The colour that endures is grey. It is like Rilke's emigrant ship: fade to grey. 'Only extinction persists', Montale writes elsewhere in Le Occasioni: it's really not a cheerful book. What begins as an Impressionist idyll with straw hats and gondolier shirts, ends with concrete boots, in the Hackensack marshes in New Jersey. The poem has stopped collecting; it has gone through its abstract, algebraical phase ('the great turmoil/ great repose'), now it is strictly payback time. The dreamings have acquired a different character in point of colour and pleasantness. It is as though the sun has abruptly gone down in the poem, the bright colours are gone, and there is a sudden chill in the air (perhaps manifest in those 'mists along the bank'), and you suddenly think about getting home and making yourself a cup of tea.

Abruptly rousing itself from those mists, the consciousness returns. It has been impolite, inattentive, wrapped up in itself, ignoring its 'tu', its talk-to. 'Another day,/ you were saying—what were you saying?' Perhaps she said, What a perfect day, or Thank God, that's another one gone, or You never listen to a single word I say. Whatever it was, it's lost on him, another day that he won't get back. It's the moment when the 'I' figure wakes up out of its reverie, as Yeats says in 'Towards Break of Day', 'the cold blown spray in my nostril'. He seems to have gone past all the landmarks or watermarks, the river has become a sort of conveyor belt, a caterpillar track, they are past everything, in darkness and emptiness. He echoes her questions with another one of his own, in difficult, elusive, almost abstract terms. A Montale speciality. 'Eastbourne' has him thinking about 'the long/ inching sea tide/ of my life, too good on the rise', 'troppo dolce sulla china'. Here it's: 'And where/ does it take us, the river mouth gathering in a single/ rush?'

Galassi has: 'And where does it lead, this mouth that seethes/ in a single stream?' A river is a road, with fewer alternatives. One imagines their little boat on a suddenly more muscular and inescapable Marne, much wider and faster, maybe among ocean-going vessels. Or, to use a terrifying image I remember from a Hugo Hamilton novel: a couple in a car at night, somehow missing all the warning signs and barriers, and carrying on down an unfinished motorway viaduct to their doom. That's the feeling of these lines: '*E dove porta/ questa bocca che brulica in un getto/ solo?*' Spat out of a mouth. Maybe by those masters of public address and wireless: Hitler, Mussolini.

Then there's something arguably settling. Where once we had '*Il sogno è questo*', 'This is the dream', now we have '*La sera è questa*', 'This is the evening'. The dream is lost; gone. The day is gone too. Present, past, replaced. The river giveth, and the river taketh away. Now it's all that's left, invisibly transporting the couple to the stars, which have come twinkling out. It is like the end of a story from Ovid's *Metamorphoses*, the man a villain or unfortunate or demigod who exceeded his prerogative, the heroine snatched away, and prettily constellated. She is a bear now, or a tree, or a star. The poem is made from all-natural ingredients. Maybe cork. A cork on a coloured corkboard. It has captured time, not one moment, but change, the change in the day, the change in the years. The sun is quite gone, and there is no more mention of the pallid moon that accompanied it. And below, an expansion of the poem's title, like a beautifully cadenced footnote-cum-dedication-cum-Impressionist-painting-title: '(*Barche sulla Marna, domenicali, in corsa/ nel dì della tua festa*).' The balance of Sunday and feast-day; Sunday and race (if indeed there was any racing going on); of '*corsa*' and '*festa*'. It, too, is settling in its factuality, its resumption of known or half-known data, a time, a place; the same thing happens in the sixth of the Motets, *'La speranza di pure rivederti/ m'abbandonava'*, 'The hope of even seeing you again/ was slipping from me', which ends with a little factual codicil, again in brackets: '(At Modena, among the porticoes,/ a flunky in gold braid was tugging/ two jackals on a leash).'[20] Montale writes: 'The parentheses were intended to isolate the example and suggest a different tone of voice, the jolt of an intimate and distant memory.'[21] As here.

Looking back, what do we see? A poem, maybe, that begins in 1933 and ends in 1937. One that starts with a happy cork, and ends, at least in Arrowsmith's English version, with 'floating'; alternatively, in the original, that goes from *'felicità'* to *'festa'*. In the course of which the river has been discoloured and widened and even tilted up like a gun barrel and levelled at the stars. One that seems to pick up symbols and values wherever it looks: a dragon, a rat; an oriole's nest, a starling; cinnabar, grey; a cork, a star; a passive benign to a malignant errancy. The complex of parallels, the subtle and seemingly 'real' arrangements of detail, give one the feeling one has read something far longer, maybe a novel. Downstream looks like downhill. You get off the river four years later, and it's too late. You are Rip Van Winkle, you go to sleep after one war, and wake up just in time for the next. Like 'Eastbourne'—the *Bank Holiday*, the *'dì della tua festa'*, the couple among strangers, the taking in of the unfamiliar scene, the embers of the day, the last of the light, the descending chill—it has an aura of helter-skelter, of curdled fun, of a dead-certain but still anguished pessimism.[22] Alternatively, or additionally, it ends in a sky-in-river parallel universe. Perhaps the poem does after all have its concealed personal component. Looking down, dejected, Montale looks away from one thing, one setting, one context, one person, and is bounced, drawn, compelled, to another. '*scendere*' and '*s'accenda*', it says in the original, '*Ora possiamo/ scendere fino a che s'accenda l'Orsa*', a tear, a disjunction, a play, that Arrowsmith rather pitifully loses: 'Now we can descend/ downstream where the Great Bear is shining.' Galassi catches it, the rivenness, but composes it, reconciles it, makes it sound leisurely and enjoyable, a bask, a breeze: 'now we can float until the Dipper rises.' When actually, it is *reculer pour mieux sauter*. Drifting down to rise up. One star rises, another falls. *Anrufung des Grossen Bären* is the title of one of Ingeborg Bachmann's poetry volumes, an appeal or summons to the Great Bear. The Bear is the North. The Bear is Connecticut or New York or New England. It is Brandeis. Irma is, to all intents and purposes, Ursa. John McPhee spent three years travelling in Alaska and takes himself to task for never having bothered to look up the word 'Arctic'.[23] 'Pertaining to, or situated under, the northern constellation called the Bear', it says. The river, the Marne, points north. Oh, my blue river baby. Montale is habitually indecisive, dithery. What the Germans call *entscheidungsschwach*—weak in decisions. He is Arsenio, not Ursenio. He offers Irma the novel with the four variant endings. 'For weeks', as the equally indecisive, equally dithery Lowell writes, but so much less obliquely, rather in the manner of a helpful patient, 'my heart has pointed elsewhere'. Montale is so much harder to treat.

KAREN SOLIE

'The World'

When I learned I could own a piece of The World
I got my chequebook out. Eternal life belongs to those
who live in the present. My wife's bright eye affirmed it.
As do the soothing neutral tones and classic-contemporary
décor of our professionally designed apartments,
private verandahs before which the globe, endlessly
and effortlessly circumnavigated, slips by, allowing residents
no ends of exotic ports, a new destination every few days
to explore with a depth we hadn't thought possible.
It's not how things are on The World that is mystical,
not the market and deli, proximity of masseuse
and sommelier, not the gym, our favourite restaurant,
our other favourite restaurant, the yacht club, the library,
the golf pro, the pool, but that it exists at all, a limited
whole, a logic and a feeling. What looks like freedom
is, in fact, the perfection of a plan, and property
a stocktaking laid against us in a measure. The difference
between a thing thought, and done. One can ignore neither
the practical applications nor the philosophical significance
of our onboard jewelry emporium, its $12 million inventory,
natural yellow diamonds from South Africa no one needs,
thus satisfying the criteria for beauty. Without which
there is no life of the mind. What we share, though, transcends
ownership, our self-improvement guaranteed

by the itineraries, licensed experts who prepare us
for each new harbour and beyond, deliver us into the hands
of native companions on The World's perpetual course.
The visual field has no limits. And the eye—
the eye devours. Polar bears, musk oxen, rare thick-billed
murre. We golfed on the tundra and from The World
were airlifted to pristine snowfields, clifftops where we dined
alfresco above frozen seas. The World is the entirety.
The largest ship ever to traverse the Northwest Passage.
How the silent energy coursed between us. Fundamental rules
had changed. Except, with time, it seems a sort of accident—
natural objects combined in states of affairs, their internal
properties. Accusatory randomness and proliferation
of types, brutal quantity literally brought to our doors.
Or past them, as if on the OLED high-def screen
of our circumstances, which hides more than it reveals.
For what we see could be other than it is.
Whatever we're able to describe at all could be other
than it is. Such assaults on our finer feelings require an appeal
to order, to the exercise of discipline a private Jacuzzi represents,
from which one might peacefully enjoy the singular euphoria
of the Panama Canal or long-awaited departure
from fetid Venice. There is some truth in solipsism, but I fear
I'm doing it wrong, standing at the rail for ceremonial cast-offs
thunderously accessorized with Vangelis or 'Non, je ne regrette rien',
made irritable by appreciative comments about the light.
In Reykjavik or Cape Town, it's the same. Familiarity
without intimacy is the cost of privacy, security
of a thread count so extravagant its extent can no longer
be detected. Even at capacity, The World is eerily empty:
its crew of highly trained specialists in housekeeping,
maintenance, beauty, and cuisine—the heart and soul
of the endeavour—are largely unseen and likely where the fun is.
We sit at the captain's table but don't know him. He's Italian.
I think on my Clarksville boyhood long before EPS, ROE—
retractable clothesline sunk in concrete, modest backyard
a staging ground for potential we felt infinite to the degree

our parents knew it wasn't. The unknown is where we played.
And while fulfilment of a premeditated outcome
confers a nearly spiritual comfort of indifference
to the time of year, a paradise of fruits always in season,
the span of choice defines its limit, which cannot be exceeded.
The sea rolls over, props on an elbow, and now is heard
the small sound of a daydream running softly aground.
Dissatisfaction, in a Danish sense. On prevailing winds a scent
of compromise; for one tires of the spacewalk outside
what is the case. Beyond immediate luxuries
lives speculation and the tragic impression one is yet
to be born. It could be when all pursuits have been satisfied,
life's problems will remain untouched. But doubt exists only
where questions exist. The World satisfies its own conditions.
It argues for itself. Herein lies an answer.[1]

What's this, then? Something massy and immoderate, as seamless and imposing as the thing it describes. A great shining tower of contemporary glibspeak. A commercial message from a sponsor, given in the husky caramel of an actor. It might have been pharmaceuticals or litigation, SUVs or fast food. A political candidate's 'personal narrative' or anonymized screed. A poem barely a year or two behind the investment brochure of the thing it describes: a moveable timeshare. 'Modern and normal', to apply the title of the second book of poems by Karen Solie, Canadian, born in Moose Jaw, Saskatchewan, in 1967. In other words, an air-conditioned nightmare. Handily at the cutting edge of a number of recent financial, industrial, ecological, and societal developments. Four pages, no breaks, long lines, conventional punctuation, lower case at the margins. Style: a sort of elite jargon. In the context of poetry, a piece of solid engineering, the equivalent of an unparagraphed Thomas Bernhard novel. Imagine the turning circle on this baby. Launched by the champagne of its first sentence that bubbles through a line and a half:[2] 'When I learned I could own a piece of The World/ I got my chequebook out.' Who's not on board with that. Anapaests, rising metre—learned, own, piece, World—quenched by the clobbering stresses on cheque, book and out. 'When I earned I could loan', 'When I loaned I could earn', the spoonerish/malapropish variants in the background, offering deformation. 'The World' upper case, but not italicized. It would seem the author has some interest in perpetuating the equivocation; but *verbum sap.*, we are not talking about the third planet from the sun here. Or not primarily anyway.

I've described poetry as the controlled release of information. It's no different here. What do we learn? That the speaker—married, and presumably a man (jumping ahead to line 3)—is interested in learning; that he is in fact a very literal participant in, to coin a phrase, the knowledge economy. 'learned' infers knowledge and 'own' brings in economy. That the word 'piece' has grown latterly to equal or almost exceed the whole. 'Some', here, is more than 'all': a piece of the action, a piece of ass, a piece of pie. (Or, alternatively, a piece of piss, a piece of work, a piece of shit.) But it keeps its air of understatement, false modesty, vengefulness, entitlement. It's actually sort of PC, believe it or not. Even though, 'a piece of The World'—the sound of that!—it must be at the very least a continent. That the speaker doesn't sit around—actually, he does, but never mind that now!—but acts on his hunches. That nothing talks like money—which as we know is speech, ever since Citizens United (which, come to think of it is just about as glorious and vainglorious and self-glorying a name as The World), with First Amendment protection—or that the having of money confers proportionate or maybe disproportionate licence to talk.

Take a bow, Koch brothers, and sundry super PACs. Here is a venture capitalist. A venturesome capitalist. An adventure capitalist. An Adventist capitalist. A windy, loquacious capitalist. A capitalist who likes his blue skies thinking pushing the envelope and outside the box. One thinks of Marvell and his coy mistress, 'had we but world enough, and time,/ this coyness, lady were no crime'.

And lo, hot on the heels of The World comes 'eternal life'. A further usufruct. And another major preoccupation of wealth. The yen for cryogenics, for banked cells, for slight return, for Chapter Eleven immortality and Fitzgerald's *quondam* impossible, now routine, second act. Our speaker has the world, and, it seems time—seventy-six lines!—and is not troubled by any coyness. 'My wife's bright eye affirmed it.' Perhaps last of the major lessons, that this World is an MS, a ship, a luxury cruise-ship, which fact slips, a little obliquely, out of 'circumnavigated' in line 7 and 'exotic ports' in line 8, and a little whimsically, from the 'depth' of the exploration of line 9. But it's not shouted from the rooftops. Oddly, for such a long boast and flaunt, there's some discretion here. You could vary the old modesty joke and say, 'Discretion is a great quality. I have it.'

I seem to remember that when I first read the poem, I thought this 'World' thingy was an invention. It seemed simply too good to be true. Stop The World, I want to get off! Or now, on. Something so exclusive and exclusionary. A community not spiritual or social or familial or even intellectual, but sybaritic, numismatic, plutocratic. Where the resident passenger proprietors have taken a vow not of poverty but of wealth. A blatantly wonderful meta-phor for the detachment of the super-rich, for 'widening income inequality', itself a sort of wandering parasite skating over the wet part of the world's surface, and an ideal locale for the contemporary transactional transnational, the pampered billionaire sociopath, the member of the rootless elite who use their wallets for passports, and change their nationalities, to vary Brecht, oftener than their shoes. They flash an Aesculapian harmlessness at us, more or less like some other well-travelled creatures in Solie's collection: 'The pine beetle and rusty grain beetle/ don't realize the harm they do, they are only having experiences.'³ Accordingly, I took the whole thing for a verbal political fantasy of Solie's. The mobility of goods, services, of course capital, and a few individuals. Not at all. A 'Note' to her 2015 book in which the poem first appears, *The Road In Is Not the Same Road Out*, has it: 'The World of "The World" is a cruise liner of 165 luxury apartments owned by a community of residents who live on board as it continuously sails the globe. The poem also draws from Ludwig Wittgenstein's *Tractatus Logico-Philosophicus*.' The reference to Wittgenstein makes me nervous, Cambridge man and all. I hope to return to it later on, but I can tell you already, you won't be hearing much about him.

I have seen vaguely abusive-seeming photographs of cruise-ships tied up in front of St. Mark's in Venice (it looks, forgive me, something like the '70s band Slade in their platform shoes stepping in dogshit); seen one in the metal in Roseau, Dominica, where their one- or two-hour layovers compress the productive day for beggars and street-sellers and everyone else to a similar patch of time, and give rise to vicious little traffic jams; heard the festive foghorns and seen the fireworks of gratitude when one chooses to put in to Hamburg. They make, basically, a cargo cult of our entire planet. They are money, money aptly with a screw and a mate, with an anchor and a purser. We are there for them with out-stretched hands, with outstretched ears. When, some months or years later, I looked the thing up on Wiki, 'MS The World', I saw some things familiar from the poem, and others not: that it is the world's largest privately owned residential yacht; that it was built in Norway and Sweden; that it has twelve decks and six restaur-ants; that it is flagged from the Bahamas, and operated from Miramar, Florida, and by some people called ResidenSea; that its average occupancy is 150–200 residents and guests, and its crew numbers approximately 280; that the Northwest Passage sailing alluded to in the poem in fact took place in 2012; that a cross-referenced article is headlined 'Shrinking ice makes Nunavut more accessible to cruise ships, but money stays on board' (sur-prise, surprise); that 'See also' offers links to 'Utopia (cruise ship)', a similar resident-owned vessel under construction, and also 'Seasteading, the concept of creating permanent dwellings at sea'.

As I say, I first supposed 'The World' was invention; not so. But nor is it pure research either. Karen Solie kindly took the trouble to write to me:

'The World' began here in St. John's. . . . The ship, The World, docked in the harbour, and the way I recall it, as I was puzzling over its name, the rear end opened and excreted some little yachts, which went beetling off towards The Narrows, but that might have been a dream. A lot of cruise ships dock here, and usually there are people crawling all over them, and music, noise, and lights. A little trashy, sure, but lively. But The World I remember as strangely quiet, like a house with all the curtains drawn in the day, little yachts notwith-standing. Its inhabitants may have all been off on dramatic excur-sions, who knows.[4]

This initial vision—real or dream-enhanced—led Solie to pursue the thing online, to read some of its—what else—literature. There she found out more:

> The World is not for me. The World looks like something that seemed a good idea at the time. A can-implies-ought scenario. The feeling of an endpoint to it, a culmination, having acquired so much money and so many things and now all that's left is to sit in the jacuzzi or lie in bed or drink in the terrifying lounge as the real world goes by, a movement without effort, without imagination, without risk. No more questions on The World, it is the answer. All the places have been seen, all needs met, all goals achieved, all mysteries satisfied in the tourist mode, acquiring destinations and experiences, checking off the list, which is then framed and hung on the wall of one's increasingly dated condo. The décor seems to me hideous, cloying, claustrophobic. Like handbags that are uglier the more expensive they are. Difference a commodity experienced as sameness....I imagine The World's opulence deteriorating, its decor and inhabitants shabbier and more anachronistic by the year, the pages of the calendar flapping by....My own class anxieties and prejudices are part of the way I view The World. Though, still, it screams to me waste, exploitation, Neil Diamond medleys, and norovirus....A lot like the real world.[5]

I hope you'll agree, her description is just as virtuosic and alive as the poem itself. But how consoling and old-fashioned to think that there was a personal encounter at the base of it. It's not just a pressed flower out of a book, someone first sniffed it for us.

It would be perfectly possible for a poem like 'The World' to be documentary and *veriste*, to live from its exorbitant details and make us, its readers, gasp or vomit with envy or visceral horror at this cross between Noah's Ark and the Nautilus; ghost-ship and social housing; a shark and a space-station; the Flying Dutchman and a gated mall; tireless, immiserating, stocked to the gills and barely there. The curtains drawn, indeed. As Rimbaud says in his 'Drunken Boat', 'a martyr of the latitudes and poles'. And there *are* the details, the private verandahs and the exotic ports, our favourite restaurant and our other favourite restaurant, the golf pro and the pool, Reykjavik and Venice, the paradise of fruits always in season. (Who are these fruits, you ask yourself.) But there is a whole other plane of regard (as Brodsky used to say) and type of vocabulary: 'mystical', 'freedom', 'philosophical significance', 'life of the mind', 'perpetual', 'pristine', 'entirety', 'fundamental', 'infinite', 'spiritual', 'tragic'. 'Dissatisfaction, in a Danish sense.' These—and many more besides—are all abstract, absolute, testing limits, horizon words. It is as though the poem were on the cusp of physical and metaphysical, at the freezing point where the real becomes an idea, which is something that inheres in the great poems and stories of sea and shipping, because at some point all voyages have to be ideas first or after: the *Odyssey* and *Moby Dick*, *Two Years before the Mast* and *20,000 Leagues under the Sea*, *Arthur Gordon Pym* and *Le Bateau Ivre*, Wallace Stevens's *The Comedian as the Letter C* and Katherine Anne Porter's *Ship of Fools*, Malcolm Lowry's *Ultramarine* and James Buchan's *High Latitudes*.

In the same way, Solie's speaker is not simply a businessman or a retiree—though he may be either one or both—but also a thinker. He is someone who lives on deck and in his stateroom—or securely behind his ding-a-ling front door—but also in his head. He is a cruise-ship explainer, conversant with the details from the brochurage, and a whizz at the style, but like Odysseus and Crispin, or Ahab and Nemo, he is a mental voyager as well, the obnoxious coupon-cutter with added extras, the businessman listening to the good angel perched on his right shoulder—on his left there is a chip. (Besides, there's actually no really compelling reason for him to be a possible speaker; in the context of a poem, he could just as well be an impossible one: the Earth Spirit, a tomato, a neutrino, the girl under the stairs. In other words, he could be merged or schizo, an aria or a duet. Like Rimbaud, half-boy, half-boat.) Perhaps for a thinking poet like Solie, the category of the unthinking or thoughtless is just intrinsically untempting. Why go there? It's perhaps too easy. The nineteenth-century poet A.H. Clough wrote about the modern Hamlet with a railway time-table. In the twenty-first why not give Prospero a permanent billet on a residential yacht and the intelligence and scrupulousness of his maker, Shakespeare or Solie? The poem goes from learning—that he could own a piece of The World—to finding, or contending that he has found—the words on which the poem ends—'an answer'. How to live? What to do? Why to be? The speaker is interested in the conversion from physical to ideational and back again. The poem has ambitions beyond taking down the hubristic naming of one particular, over-accoutred boat; its interrogation, its questioning fire is also directed at the thinking that engendered it and that it in turn engenders. 'The World' is a comedy of style, but also a comedy of substance, and vice versa. It is a thought experiment. The mind, the ship, the world, these are fractals. What is going on on the planet, it asks, and also, what is going on inside people's heads. What is possession? What is acquisition? What is availability? Is it the task of the poet still—as Rilke thought—to name the things of this world for the benefit of the angels ('house,/ bridge, fountain, gate, pitcher, fruit-tree, window')[6] as though they were so many specifications conferring so much value; or not perhaps by now, to un-name them? To go from the particular to the general, the concrete to the abstract, the fine point to the implication. Nothing else in the poem has quite the status of the line 'Polar bears, musk oxen, rare thick-billed/ murre', because these alone, though promised, and so to speak, on the menu, cannot be guaranteed; they have the power to take themselves off, to no-show. They, while touted and objectified, are not necessarily there. Their pursuits may not be compatible with ours; the lines quite simply might not intersect. 'thick-billed/ murre.' These bills are for once not dollars.

The poem makes a sort of dance between the concrete and the abstract, between the caricature and the unanswerable, between the rapacious and the worried. 'I got my chequebook out', then 'Eternal life belongs to those who live in the present'. 'we dined alfresco above frozen seas' and 'The World is the entirety'. 'the OLED high-def screen' (which I need to look up) and 'what we see could be other than it is'. And the voice moves along, from brochure and fact and enticement and swank to speculation and musing. It's not particularly obvious, but the thing swings from side to side, like a pendulum, like a metronome, like a windscreen wiper. 'natural yellow diamonds from South Africa', and 'which no one needs,/ thus satisfying the criteria for beauty. Without which/ there is no life of the mind.' This puts the poem and the voice always at the point where both are changing state—a freezing point, a melting point, a boiling point. The poem is both a physical and a metaphysical instancing and critique. By giving her speaker a higher mind and a philosophical cast, Solie creates more and bigger instability. What horizons are these? What is the vision here? What kind of life is this that offers 165 residences? What contact with freedom or infinity is provided? Why not spite Bunuel, cut out the middleman and eat on the toilet—and is there any greater pleasure? One could imagine a similar approach taken by or with the coming hawkers of space travel, Elon Musk or Richard

Branson. Having sold us their cars and trains, they are now selling us their ideas.

As I say, I think it would work if it wasn't, if it simply coasted on subject, but there it is: philosophical, thoughtful, existential, whatever you want to call it. The speaker comes with spare capacity, max headroom. The thought is self-delighting, or accidentally self-immiserating, like those spinning columns of water described by Elizabeth Bishop, in her 'Crusoe in England':

> And I had waterspouts. Oh,
> half a dozen at a time, far out,
> they'd come and go, advancing and retreating,
> their heads in cloud, their feet in moving patches
> of scuffed-up white.
> Glass chimneys, flexible, attenuated,
> sacerdotal beings of glass…I watched
> the water spiral up in them like smoke.

Thought volatilizes like money, goes shopping, goes AWOL, switches liquescently here and there, swells and slumps, buys in and out. 'My wife's bright eye affirmed it'—as though she was a hawk or a wolverine, something from nature. A strangely impersonal manner, paired with those familiar, calamitous rhythms of boom and bust. Crisis-prone, as Karl Marx once noted. 'How the silent energy coursed between us.' A sagging boast. The sentences put out more sail in terms of qualifiers and modifiers, achieve ever more balanced seaworthiness in the form of grammatical outriggers and catamarans and double hulls and centreboards; and then slump periodically into the wreckage of terse aphorisms:

> It's not how things are on The World that is mystical,
> not the market and deli, proximity of masseuse

and sommelier, not the gym, our favourite restaurant,
our other favourite restaurant, the yacht club, the library,
the golf pro, the pool, but that it exists at all, a limited
whole, a logic and a feeling. What looks like freedom
is, in fact, the perfection of a plan, and property
a stocktaking laid against us in a measure. The difference
between a thing thought, and done.

We go through the marvellously upholstered blandishments that
swell the sentence between line 2 and line 5: the really lush, jin-
gling convenience music of 'proximity' and 'gym'; the French
pairing of 'masseuse' (I confess, I always hope for the American
pronunciation, mass-ooss) and 'sommelier'; the humble, terres-
trial 'market' and 'deli' (both of them strongly implying streets);
the lovely joke on 'our favourite restaurant' and 'our other favourite
restaurant'; then the crossed absurdities of having a 'yacht club'
and a 'pool' on board, like an island on a lake, yes, like Yeats's 'Lake
Isle', because all this is another modest idyll, another home from
home for the burrowing hermits of Londonistan; and the different
absurdities of that dowdiest form of entertainment, the 'library',
and that snazziest and most optimistic of employees, the 'golf
pro'. But then it's none of the above, so strike the sails, cancel the
praeteritio, scale down and batten down, it's 'that it exists at all'
that is mystical. 'a limited whole', something perfect in every
detail, containing everything (un)necessary, like a cell or a seed.
A logic—maybe Occam's—and a feeling—fractals. Small is beau-
tiful, a *multum in parvo*, or indeed a whole *Minimundus*, with
thigh-high Eiffel Tower and Taj Mahal and Colosseum and the
rest of them. 'freedom' is in fact 'the perfection of a plan' and
'property' 'a stocktaking laid against us in a measure'—which I
think means depreciation, amortization. You use it *and* lose it, both.

'The difference between a thing thought, and done'—*caveat emptor* and repent at leisure.

The moral of the book title, *The Road In Is Not the Same Road Out*—perhaps that is the course or the trajectory taken by 'The World'. You board in a hurry, and then stay behind (curtains drawn) to bounce off the walls and puke into the sofas. Luxury and liberty turn out to be either offensively small or thoroughly misleading (or mis-sold?) categories. The boastful descriptive voice ties itself in knots of bafflement, reaches its horizons, is beaten back. 'The World is the entirety', it says. But then, with the banality of a pub quiz, 'The largest ship ever to traverse the Northwest Passage'. Within its sentences, the voice is commodious, urbane, expansive, at home. But it is the difficulty of making a new one that is repeatedly striking, as witness the number of verbless sentences. Or the ones that pick up and walk back or ramify or expand on what has just been said, that begin, 'Without which', or 'Except, with time', or 'Or past them'. The details seem to teeter on the brink of redundancy: 'soothing' and 'neutral', 'décor' and 'designed', or wittily, 'alfresco' and 'frozen'. Always implicit within this luxury padding is the fear of silence, the fear of running out—of experiences, of advantages, of unique selling-points. It is a desire to think big but out of a context of defensiveness, from within a circumstantial knot of privilege and anxiety and timetable. Trying to live down the upper-case W in 'World', or pretend it wasn't there. Living heedlessly, without responsibilities ('We sit at the captain's table but don't know him. He's Italian'), in the simulacrum of the pure consumption version that we have been told in our time that life now is.

What is surprising and keeps the poem alive—because a poem is a *perpetuum mobile*, with both the fuel and the instability to keep it going—is the way even this document of privilege shares something of the unease ('Dissatisfaction, in a Danish sense') of speakers in other Solie poems having to reckon with the ordinary dismalness, unpredictability and general grot of contemporary, terrestrial life in Canada, America, Britain; the ones that are pre-occupied with bedbugs ('Be Reasonable'), that grew up in a failed town ('Keebleville'), or remember touring the Grand Canyon with the wrong man in a dodgy motor ('The Road In Is Not the Same Road Out') or scout out manky apartments ('Conversion'). I'll quote something I wrote about Solie a couple of years back, when I first tried:

> A poem of Solie's is sentences in unpredictable but deep sequence in unpredictable but braced lines. It seems out of control, but isn't; it exhibits grace while falling, which is perhaps what grace is. It runs the gamut from nervous, garrulous charm to the glory and shear of impersonal style: it is idiomatic splicing in one voice. It offers wisdom, fact and bitter experience.[7]

In 'The World', if you didn't know where you were as reader, you could quite easily remain in ignorance, in lines like:

> There is some truth in solipsism, but I fear
> I'm doing it wrong, standing at the rail for ceremonial cast-offs
> thunderously accessorized with Vangelis or 'Non, je ne regrette rien',
> made irritable by appreciative comments about the light.

Vangelis, the Greek demi-god of the early synthesizer, Piaf, the French nightingale. He hardly sounds like one of the chosen (or self-selected) First 165. Any more than he does in the poem's single sepia flashback (remember Rimbaud's boat, hankering for the ramparts of Europe!):

> I think on my Clarksville boyhood long before EPS, ROE—
> retractable clothesline sunk in concrete, modest backyard
> a staging ground for potential we felt infinite to the degree
> our parents knew it wasn't. The unknown is where we played.

'EPS' is 'earnings per share', 'ROE' is 'return on equity'. The retractable clothesline is this Citizen Kane's Rosebud, the knowledge nowhere or even disabling. What I think here is that the speaker has perhaps internalized something of the flux and unknowability of the sea. Either that, or he has failed to generate the requisite marine consciousness. For all the q.v. Seasteading and the endless amenities, he is at some level homesick, and has a sense of having followed the wrong fork ('There is some truth in solipsism, but I fear/ I'm doing it wrong'). His thoughts don't have the earthbound stability and vauntingness one would expect of them, and of him. Waves wash over him. The uncertain element has somehow infected him, in all his capitalist bullishness. If people had been meant to live in The World, maybe we would have been given fins and gills, which, come to think of it, is how we started out a long time ago.

Having, like Archimedes, somewhere to stand and a pivot, Solie can move the world. Or even The World. Her speaker is on board, at least with the project, but ill at ease; 'thunderously accessorized' but 'made irritable' like Jove; 'at capacity' and 'eerily empty'. He is orotund but Pyrrhic. Sentences stuffed with 'brutal quantity' don't hide the fact that the place and the basis for it have something actually hellish about them. The poem keeps running into whorls of pessimistic understanding, things that are grave, desolating, unalterable. In the current American term of art, negative:

'Without which/ there is no life of the mind.'

'The visual field has no limits.'

'Fundamental rules/ had changed.'

'Familiarity/ without intimacy is the cost of privacy.'

'The span of choice defines its limit, which cannot be exceeded.'

The possibility of everything leads to an oddly trammelled existence, the absence of prohibition or impediment or limit to a small and rather peevish, anxious consciousness. The presence of so much infinity makes one feel—well, actually, small. We are frankly bored, bored and in the territory of Sophocles' chorus in *Antigone*:

> There are many wonders on this earth
> and man has made the most of them;
> though only death has baffled him
> he owns the universe, the stars,
> *sput* satellites and great societies.
>
> Fish pip inside his radar screens
> and foals kick out of a syringe:
> he bounces on the dusty moon
> and chases clouds about the sky
> so they can dip on sterile ground.

(The downbeat, contemporary-dated version is from Tom Paulin).[8] It is the 'can-implies-ought scenario', as Solie put it, the thing that drags us kicking and screaming into the inequity and alienation we call the future. But who can live on the cutting edge? This sort of Lucullan life, the incessant calibration of experience, its pricing, its numbering and notching, the supplying of bar-codes for it, leads to its disappearance; we have the foot-rule without the fish. Life's problems, as the poem says, 'will remain untouched'. The de-contextualization of everything is a prequel to its withering; you look for the word 'marble' to appear in the poem, and when it doesn't, you strangely don't miss it. Solie's musing passenger/ co-proprietor is actually a variant of Persephone, The World a type of Hell—'like Purgatory', as the poet wrote to me in her email. The ungrateful upshot of so many months of hyper-educational, connoisseurial stops ('fetid Venice', 'in Reykjavik or Cape Town, it's the same') and so many thousands of miles of privileged, purposeless churning is 'the tragic impression one is yet/ to be born'. No better than a happy ancient Greek. Indeed, so many treats and so much solicitude seem likely to have had something infantilizing about them all along. The 'Herein lies an answer' might as well be 'Now let us pray'. A poem extolling an Epicurean whizzbang of excess ends up as a text of stoicism. Gritted teeth. Outthrust jaw. Please no sympathy. The sea propped, again like an ancient Greek, or Roman, 'on an elbow'. As Rilke wrote, 'who speaks of victory; surviving is all'.

CONCLUSION

I have explained how the idea for these talks and this book first came to me, sitting on the little sofa-raft in our room in Hamburg one evening in the summer of 2017, and suddenly having an overwhelming sense of Rilke's '*Auswanderer-Schiff*'; thinking 'more boats, more boats'; and quite quickly coming up with the rest of the *galère*, Rimbaud, Montale, and Solie. I was a little surprised Sylvia Plath's 'On Deck' wasn't among them. Les Murray's own 'Emigrant Ship', called 'Immigrant Voyage' ('My wife came out on the *Goya*/ in the mid-year of our century') was another attractive possibility. But that would have made the enterprise too English, or too Anglophone, and I liked the chance balance of languages. The idea of these ships was the first thought I'd had in months that broke the spell of Brexit (though it would certainly like to be a rejection of Brexit by other means). The principle of *Messing About in Boats* is the Schengen principle. It is that poems, and an interest in poems, like goods and services and human beings, should be able to travel freely.

Of course, I wasn't thinking strategically, I don't really hold with strategic thought, just flipping over cards: I'm not much of a believer in the operation of choice or choosing, in any case, in human affairs. But no sooner alighted on than immediately justified. So my quartet commended itself to me almost from the start, for its balance. Four languages—even though, as I say, this was not intended. Different lengths, from Rilke's sonnet extent—*mas o menos*—to Rimbaud's one hundred lines. Different ages, from Rimbaud's nineteenth-century modern classic, to Solie's twenty-first. Different prominence, from Rimbaud to Montale. Differences in recessiveness or availability. Above all, I liked the idea of having my attention compelled by relatively brief forms. Literature to me has always been more to do with intensity than extensiveness.

Nor did I particularly think of the poems in relation to each other, as covering the same ground, so to speak, or different ground; the same water, or different water. Here, too, I think I was lucky. Rilke's ship, never leaving port, being loaded up, and finally sinking under the weight of the poet's disapproval. Rimbaud's, disencumbered, unmanned, eventually turning into pure light, pure colour, pure geography. Solie's like a peopled version of Rimbaud's, and hence (the boat, not the poem) banal or doubly ghostly. And Montale's, a small boat, a rowboat, a pleasure boat, a river boat, and then a star-ship. Perhaps all voyages and all vessels are a type—only one doesn't know in advance what the type is, Ark or Bismarck, Titanic or Nautilus, Ultramarine or Purple Passage. Two static voyages—the Rilke and the Montale, which seems to have the banks towed past it—and two never-stopping, the Rimbaud and the Solie. Boats with no passengers, with two, with a hundred-and-fifty-odd, with thousands. Guy Davenport writes: 'From Noah's ark to Jonah's storm-tossed boat out of Joppa to the Roman ships in which Saint Paul sailed perilously, the ship in history has always been a sign of fate itself.' And just as fateful, to set foot in poems, the uncertain element.

NOTES

Introduction

1. Paul Muldoon, 'Profumo'.
2. '"No interesting project can be embarked on without fear. I shall be scared to death half the time." Sir Francis Chichester in Sydney'.
3. Author of the magisterial study, *The Poem Itself*, 1960.

Chapter 1

1. *Letters of R.M. Rilke, 1892–1910*, tr. Green and Herter Norton, p. 47.
2. Quoted in Rilke, *The Notebooks of Malte Laurids Brigge*, tr. Burton Pike, p. 39.
3. *Letters*, p. 108.
4. Quoted on p. 72 in my *Behind the Lines*.
5. See ibid., p. 70, observing that *Malte* is generally viewed as critically/disdainfully as the *New Poems*, and for the same reason, because it doesn't have an elevating message of the kind that is expected from Rilke.
6. Cited in ibid., p. 60.
7. Ibid., p. 28.
8. Ibid., p. 36.
9. Ibid., p. 31.
10. Rilke, *Letters on Cézanne*, tr. Joel Agee, p. 24.
11. Rilke, *Where Silence Reigns: Selected Prose*, tr. Houston, p. 105.
12. Rilke, *Letters on Cézanne*, tr. Joel Agee, p. 28.
13. 'Buddha in der Glorie' in Rilke, *New Poems [1908]: The Other Part*, tr. Snow, pp. 220–1.
14. Ibid.
15. *Letters*, p. 235.
16. Ibid., p. 237.

17. 'The Fishmonger's Stall', included in *Ahead of All Parting: The Selected Poetry and Prose of Rainer Maria Rilke*, ed. and tr. by Stephen Mitchell, p. 286.
18. *Letters*, pp. 237–8.
19. Ibid., p. 239.
20. See Snow, pp. 104–5.
21. George Schoolfield, *Young Rilke and His Time*, p. 249. See also Schoolfield's chapter 'Auswandererschiff', pp. 249–59.
22. The sort of thing that Alfred Döblin was parodying in this passage from his 1929 novel *Berlin Alexanderplatz* (my translation, p. 65):

    a pale, slender woman was lying with eyes wide open. Her dark, luxurious hair lay tangled on the silk sheets (Kerkauen Castle, renowned for its silk sheets). Shudders of cold convulsed her. Her teeth chattered as in an icy frost, full stop. She, comma, though, comma, did not draw the blankets around her, full stop. Her shapely ice-cold hands lay still (as in a deep frost, shuddering with cold, slender woman with eyes wide open, renowned silk sheets), full stop. Her shining eyes wandered flickeringly in the dark, and her quaking lips breathed, colon, open quotation marks, capital o-aitch Helena, em-dash, em-dash, close quotation marks, rotation marks, flotation marks.

23. Quoted in Schoolfield, *Young Rilke*, p. 251, excerpted and modified.
24. Ibid., p. 252.
25. 'Auswanderer-Schiff' and 'Emigrant Ship', see Snow, pp. 106–7.
26. Rilke, *New Poems*, with a translation, introduction, and notes by J.B. Leishman, pp. 226–9.
27. Mass emigration was hated and feared for all sorts of reasons, and in all sorts of quarters. Here is one, from Joseph Conrad's friend Cunninghame Graham, while Conrad worked at his *Nostromo* ('it is however concerned mostly with Italians'), drawn from Maya Jasanoff's bravura *The Dawn Watch* (p. 251):

    In a string of books and sketches published from 1895 onward, Graham portrayed South America as a place ruined by greed. He mourned *A Vanished Arcadia* in the Jesuit missions of colonial Paraguay, where priests protected Guarani Indians from near-certain enslavement by Spanish settlers and formed 'a semi-communistic settlement', sharing products of ranch and field. He grieved for 'A Vanishing Race' of gauchos, rugged individualists who were getting shoved aside 'by the heavy-footed Basque, the commonplace Canary Islander, and the Italian in his greasy velveteen suit'. In the free, open pampas of his youth, Graham could already see trains 'snort and puff' where once 'the ostrich scudded', capitalists who 'rob[bed] in counting-houses and on exchange with pen and book, instead of on the highway' at knife-point. He saw 'civilisation...plant its empty sardine tin as a mark on the earth's face...and the hideous pall of gloom and hypocrisy which generally accompanies it' blight the pampas.

28. Quoted from 'Across Siberia', in *The Unknown Chekhov*, tr. Yarmolinsky, p. 269.
29. Egon Schwartz, *Poetry and Politics in the Works of Rainer Maria Rilke*, p. 59.
30. From 'The Leviathan', in Joseph Roth, *Collected Stories* (p. 59, my translation).
31. There is nothing of the pathos and human scale that Joseph Roth brings to the subject in his 1923 piece, 'Emigrant Ship' (published in *The Hotel Years*, my translation) describing the *Pittsburgh* leaving Bremerhaven with its load of Eastern Jews bound for the US or Canada:

> The peasants' wives have the timid, flickering eyes of frightened animals as they watch the bustle, great ships' cranes taking up huge quantities of coals, slowly swivelling in mid-air, the scoops opening like giant hands, and spilling their load into the hold. They hear the unfamiliar clang of the heavy ship's bell, the warning cries of the dockers, the thunder or clatter of the rolling trucks. They see how the harbour goes on and on, offering the illimitable ocean to the eye, a never-before-seen endlessness of blue.
>
> Way up in the air the Stars and Stripes flutter over the international shipping banner, which is as blue as the sky and the sea, and with a white circle in the middle, like a perfectly regular cloud. On the bridge stands a man with his cap strapped over chin and ears, giving out orders in incomprehensible terms. His commands are as mysterious as the great sea itself. A little tug tows the ship with thick hawsers; like a willing triumphal gate the harbour locks slowly and ceremonially open. The emigrants are on board; they call out to the disappearing land. No one has come to see them off, so they wave to strangers, to the luminous policeman, to the dockers and porters. Up at the rim of a huge

chimney appears a black figure, a chimneysweep, a toy figure compared to the enormous liner, so tiny is his silhouette against the endless blue background. Out of the perfectly round windows of their cabins the emigrants' faces catch their last sight of Europe.

Roth never made such a journey himself to the New World, no more than Rilke did; and like Rilke, he is not averse to colour, to suggestion, to symbolism. He too writes in joined-up pictures, but he is on the level of the age, and he feels human sympathy with those he describes. The women with their eyes, the pilot with his hat tied on, the mysterious chimneysweep (always associated in German folklore with good fortune), the pathos of the last look back through the round—infinite— windows.

32. The letter to von Hulewicz, 13 November 1925.
33. From the poem 'On Thinking about Hell', in Bertolt Brecht, *Poems 1913–1956*, ed. Manheim and Willett, p. 367.
34. Quoted in Schoolfield, *Young Rilke*, p. 255.
35. Houston, *Where Silence Reigns*, p. 119.
36. Kathleen Komar, in her essay 'Rethinking Rilke's *Duineser Elegien* at the End of the Millennium'.
37. Schwartz, *Poetry and Politics*, p. 1.
38. Referred to by Schoolfield, *Young Rilke*, p. 258.

Chapter 2

1. Perhaps he was swayed by his title, *Rimbaud: The Double Life of a Rebel*, by Edmund White, p. 66.
2. Graham Robb, *Rimbaud*, with typical asperity, notes: 'A point made so often that it deserves to appear in a *Dictionary of Received Ideas* of literary criticism is that Rimbaud wrote "Le Bateau Ivre" without having seen the sea. One might just as well be amazed that he managed to write it without having met an inebriated boat.'
3. Ibid., p. 102.
4. Cf. Joseph Roth's description of Marseilles in *Report from a Parisian Paradise* (my translation), p. 136:

Here everything ostensibly permanent is broken up. Here, it is re-assembled again. Here, there is continual rebuilding and demolition. No time, no power, no faith, no understanding holds for ever here. What is foreign? The foreign is at hand. What is at hand? The next wave will wash it away. What is now? It's already over. What is dead? It comes bobbing up again.

5. I am reminded of something I am given to saying: 'translation is exaggeration.'
6. From an uncollected early poem by the author, '1967–71'.
7. 'Immram' by Paul Muldoon.
8. *Selected Poems and Letters of Rimbaud*, tr. Jeremy Harding and John Sturrock, pp. 59–63.
9. Robert Greer Cohn writes, in terms that lend themselves particularly well to this, if you will, masculine aspect of 'Le Bateau Ivre' as a whole: 'The attractiveness of this figure…is his utterly above-it-all dynamism; he comes only to go: what a flash!' *The Poetry of Rimbaud*, p. 25. What a flash!
10. *Imitations*, p. 77.
11. Harding and Sturrock, p. xxvi.
12. Randall Jarrell once quipped, on the subject of Lowell's propensity for writing dramatic monologues for women: who ever saw a woman like Robert Lowell; to which one has to say, yes, but who ever saw a child like Rimbaud?
13. From 'Neo-Classical Urn', *For the Union Dead*, p. 48: 'In that season of joy,/ my turtle catch/ was thirty-three,/ dropped splashing in our garden urn,/ like money in the bank,/ the plop and splash/ of turtle on turtle,/ fed raw gobs of hash ….'
14. *Imitations*, pp. 79–80.
15. As noted by Elizabeth Bishop, in whose elegy for Lowell, 'North Haven', the following lines appear (*Poems*, p. 210):

> Years ago, you told me it was here
> (in 1932?) you first discovered *'girls'*
> and learned to sail, and learned to kiss.

16. 'Santarem', p. 207, *Poems*, by Elizabeth Bishop.
17. From the poem 'Beethoven' in *History*.
18. 'The Guttural Muse', *Field Work*, p. 28.
19. This is surely an instance of Ezra Pound's wonderful designation, 'logopoiea', 'doing things with words', which he was always hard put to authenticate or instance. He cites, without examples, Propertius and Laforgue; I think Rimbaud must be full of this verbal inadvertence or mis-directing.

20. *Words in Air*, p. 338.
21. When Rimbaud was first in Paris the previous year, he was briefly arrested and possibly raped by soldiers. Enid Starkie first makes the case; Edmund White discounts it, without giving a reason; Greer Cohn takes it as given.
22. Adapted from Brodsky's poem. 'A Part of Speech'.
23. Samuel Beckett's spirited but I think over-praised translation offers 'And my eyes have fixed phantasmagoria', for line 32.
24. 2.202 of the *Tractatus*.
25. Greer Cohn, *The Poetry of Rimbaud*, p. 356.
26. Ibid., p. 354.
27. 'The Infinite', in *Imitations*, p. 25.
28. A translation of Eugenio Montale's 'l'anguilla', 'The Eel', is included in Lowell's *Imitations*.
29. Greer Cohn, *The Poetry of Rimbaud*, p. 17.
30. Ibid., p. 171.
31. Published in *Drunken Boats*, the Cahiers Series, Sylph Editions, 2007. 'Dishevelled' is Jenkins's amiable term for his alexandrines.
32. 'The Ship', *The Collected Poems of Bertolt Brecht*, tr. David Constantine, p. 171.
33. 'The drowned girl', ibid., p. 237.

Chapter 3

1. Quoted on p. 538 of *The Second Life of Art*, ed. and tr. Jonathan Galassi.
2. Ibid.
3. Lines quoted from Galassi, *Second Life*, pp. 159, 163, 183, 193, and 211 (twice).
4. Ibid., pp. 262–3.
5. Ibid., p. 221.
6. Harry Thomas, *Poems*, pp. xxxix and xl.
7. Galassi, *Second Life*, p. 508.
8. Ibid., p. 511.
9. Ibid., p. 492.
10. Ibid., p. 501.
11. Arrowsmith, *Le Occasioni*, p. 696.
12. *Lettere a Clizia*, ed. Rosanna Bettarini, Gloria Manghetti, and Franco Zabaglia. Take for example Montale's salutation to # 100, his New

Year's letter of 1936, but wrongly dated 1935, 'O my baby, my blue river baby', which may or may not be relevant to 'Barche sulla Marna'.

13. Ibid., p. 5.
14. Ibid., p. 280.
15. Thomas, *Poems*, p. xl.
16. Les Murray says, quoting his Hungarian father-in-law, 'You ride on the world-horse once', in 'Jozsef', *Learning Human*, p. 24.
17. In 'A Dialogue with Montale on Poetry' in Galassi, *Second Life*, p. 327.
18. Ibid., p. 535.
19. Murray, *Learning Human*, p. 91.
20. In the Galassi edition, it's pp. 196–7.
21. Quoted in ibid., p. 501.
22. In G.S. Fraser's aptly crushing version, included in the New Directions *Selected Poems*, the last lines go:

> Everything will seem pointless: even the strength
> That in its gritty matrix aggregates
> Living and dead, trees and rocks,
> And from you, through you, unfolds. Holidays
> Have no pity. The band expands
> Its blare of sound, in the first dusk
> An unarmed goodness spreads itself around.
> Evil conquers… The wheel does not stop:
>
> Also Thou knewest this, Lux-in-Tenebris!
>
> In this burnt quarter of sky, whence at the first
>
> Clang of bells Thou departedst, only
>
> The guttering torch remains that, already, *was*
>
> And is not, *Bank Holiday*.

23. McPhee writes, in the title piece of *Draft No. 4*, on page 166:

> I was left, in time that followed, with one huge regret. In three years of Alaska travel, research, and writing, it never occurred to me to wonder why the Arctic was called Arctic. I never thought about it until a few years after the book was published. If only I had looked in the dictionary, I would have incorporated the word's origin into the substance of the writing. This is how 'Arctic' is defined: 'Pertaining to, or situated under, the northern constellation called the Bear.'

Chapter 4

1. Karen Solie, *The Road In Is Not the Same Road Out*, pp. 18–21.
2. Nothing against opening lines or couplets, but increasingly, I've come to think that the art of the poem (propulsion, speed, coverage) is the art of the first line-and-a-half. Many of Solie's beginnings are as spectacular as this one. So (all taken from *The Road In Is Not the Same Road Out*): 'Where the question are you alright usually finds one very much/ not alright' ('The Corner'); 'Sausage makers, salt farmers, whose wives and daughters/ smoked menthols' ('Keebleville'); or: 'Nor is the twentieth century accessible/ in Edinburgh' ('The National Gallery II'); 'It rises from the North Atlantic's stacks/ as radio silence' ('Lord of Fog'). I would also cite Les Murray: 'There is nothing about it. Much science fiction is set there/ but is not about it' ('The Future'); 'To go home and wear shorts forever/ in the enormous paddocks' ('The Dream of Wearing Shorts Forever'); Robert Lowell: 'The old South Boston Aquarium stands/ in a Sahara of snow now' ('For the Union Dead'); 'The leap from three adjectives to an object/ is impossible' ('Endings'); and Thom Gunn: 'The cup of instant coffee by your bedside/ cold as the Sixties'.
3. Solie, from 'Be Reasonable', *The Road In*, p. 26.
4. Email from Karen Solie to the writer, 27 November 2018.
5. Ibid.
6. Rilke, *Duino Elegies*, IX, ll. 32–3.
7. 'All Fresh Today', review of Solie, London Review of Books, 3 April 2014.
8. Tom Paulin, 'Chorus' (from *Antigone*), *The Road to Inver*, p. 23.

ACKNOWLEDGEMENTS

I am grateful for permission to quote the following extracts.

'Emigrant-Ship' from *New Poems [1908]: The Other Part* by Rainer Maria Rilke, translated by Edward Snow. Translation copyright © 1987 by Edward Snow. Reprinted by permission of North Point Press, a division of Farrar, Straus, and Giroux.

By Rainer Maria Rilke, translated by J.B. Leishman, from *New Poems*, copyright © 1964 by The Hogarth Press. Reprinted by permission of New Directions Publishing Corp.

'The Drunken Boat' from *Selected Poems and Letters by Arthur Rimbaud*, translated by Jeremy Harding and John Sturrock. Translation, Introduction, and Notes, copyright © Jeremy Harding and John Sturrock, 2004.

Excerpts from Arthur Rimbaud, *Selected Poems and Letters*, translated by Jeremy Harding and John Sturrock. London: Penguin Classics, copyright © 2004, PRH.

Excerpt from 'Les Poètes de sept ans' ['The Poet at Seven'] by Arthur Rimbaud, translated by Robert Lowell from *Collected Poems* by Robert Lowell, copyright © 2003 by Harriet Lowell and Sheridan Lowell. Reprinted by permission of Farrar, Straus, and Giroux.

'The ship', first published in German in 1923 as 'Das Schiff' and 'The drowned girl', originally published in German in 1922 as 'Vom ertrunkenen Mädchen', translated by David Constantine, copyright © 1960 by Bertolt-Brecht-Erben/Suhrkamp Verlag. Translation copyright © 2019, 2015 by Tom Kuhn and David Constantine, from *Collected Poems of Bertolt Brecht*, by Bertolt Brecht, translated by Tom Kuhn and David Constantine. Used by permission of Liveright Publishing Corporation.

E. Montale, 'Ossi di seppia', copyright © 2015 Mondadori Libri S.p.A., Milan. Published by arrangement with the Publisher and The Italian Literary Agency.

'Boats on the Marne', copyright © 1957 by Arnoldo Mondadori Editore. Translation copyright © 1987 by William Arrowsmith, from *Collected Poems* of *Eugenio Montale 1925–1977*, by Eugenio Montale, edited by Rosanna Warren, translated by William Arrowsmith. Used by permission of W.W. Norton & Company, Inc.

Kind thanks for 'The World' and for emails to the author, to Karen Solie.

'Chorus (from *Antigone*)' in *The Road to Inver* by Tom Paulin (2011). Published by Faber and Faber Ltd.

BIBLIOGRAPHY

Rilke

J.F. Hendry: *The Sacred Threshold: A Life of Rilke*
Wolfgang Leppmann: *Rilke*
Eudo C. Mason: *Rainer Maria Rilke*
Donald Prater: *A Ringing Glass: The Life of Rainer Maria Rilke*
Rainer Maria Rilke: *New Poems [1907]*, tr. Edward Snow
Rainer Maria Rilke: *New Poems [1908]*, tr. Edward Snow
Rainer Maria Rilke: *New Poems*, tr. J.B. Leishman
Rainer Maria Rilke: *Letters on Cézanne*, tr. Joel Agee
Rainer Maria Rilke: *The Notebooks of Malte Laurids Brigge*, tr. Burton Pike
Rainer Maria Rilke: *Ahead of All Parting: The Selected Poetry and Prose*, tr. Stephen Mitchell
Rainer Maria Rilke: *Where Silence Reigns—Selected Prose*, tr. G. Craig Houston
Joseph Roth: *The Hotel Years*, tr. Michael Hofmann
George Schoolfield: *Young Rilke and His Time*
Egon Schwarz: *Poetry and Politics in the Works of Rainer Maria Rilke*, tr. David E. Wellbery
Avrahm Yarmolinsky: *The Unknown Chekhov*

Rimbaud

Elizabeth Bishop: *Poems*
Elizabeth Bishop and Robert Lowell: *Words in Air*
Bertolt Brecht: *Collected Poems*, tr. and ed. Tom Kuhn and David Constantine
Bertolt Brecht: *Poems 1913–1956*, tr. and ed. John Willett and Ralph Manheim
Robert Greer Cohn: *The Poetry of Rimbaud*
Robert Lowell: *Imitations*
Gerald Macklin: 'Drunken Boat': Samuel Beckett's translation of Arthur Rimbaud's 'Le Bateau Ivre', in *Studies in 20th Century Literature*, volume 27, issue 1, article 7

Charles Nicholl: *Somebody Else: Arthur Rimbaud in Africa 1880–1891*
Stephen Parker: *Bertolt Brecht: A Literary Life*
Arthur Rimbaud: *Selected Poems and Letters*, tr. Jeremy Harding and John Sturrock
Graham Robb: *Rimbaud: A Biography*
ed. Francis Scarfe: *Baudelaire*
Enid Starkie: *Arthur Rimbaud*

Montale

Glauco Cambon: *Eugenio Montale's Poetry*
Claire Huffman: *Montale and the Occasions of Poetry*
Eugenio Montale: *The Occasions*, tr. William Arrowsmith
Eugenio Montale: *Collected Poems*, tr. Jonathan Galassi
Eugenio Montale: *Poems*, ed. Harry Thomas
Eugenio Montale: *Lettere a Clizia*
Eugenio Montale: *The Second Life of Art: Selected Essays*, tr. Jonathan Galassi

Solie

Karen Solie: *The Living Option: Selected Poems*
Karen Solie: *The Road In Is Not the Same Road Out*
Ludwig Wittgenstein: *Tractatus Logico-Philosophicus*

INDEX

For the benefit of digital users, indexed terms that span two pages (e.g., 52–53) may, on occasion, appear on only one of those pages.